John Bethune

Baptist Misrepresentations on Baptism

with an exposure of the systematic policy of Baptist Church publications of

misquotation from infant Baptist writers, and of misrepresentation in general,

proven from Baptist and other sources

John Bethune

Baptist Misrepresentations on Baptism
with an exposure of the systematic policy of Baptist Church publications of misquotation from infant Baptist writers, and of misrepresentation in general, proven from Baptist and other sources

ISBN/EAN: 9783337260606

Printed in Europe, USA, Canada, Australia, Japan

Cover: Foto ©Lupo / pixelio.de

More available books at **www.hansebooks.com**

BAPTIST MISREPRESENTATIONS

ON

BAPTISM.

---·◆·---

THE

EARLY CHURCH HISTORY OF INFANT BAPTISM,

WITH AN EXPOSURE OF THE

SYSTEMATIC POLICY OF BAPTIST CHURCH PUBLICATIONS OF
MISQUOTATION FROM INFANT BAPTIST WRITERS,
AND OF MISREPRESENTATION IN GENERAL,

PROVEN FROM BAPTIST AND OTHER SOURCES.

BY THE

REV. JOHN BETHUNE,

Presbyterian Minister, Chesley, Ont.

TORONTO:
PRESBYTERIAN PRINTING HOUSE, 102 BAY STREET.
1876.

NOTE.

In the beginning of March and after several very distorted and unworthy anonymous accounts of our then recent and brief controversy in Chesley had appeared in some public papers from interested parties, with zealous private efforts of a like nature among neighbours unacquainted with the facts, I intimated in a local newspaper and elsewhere that I intended to publish soon the account now presented in the following pages; in consequence of which many have looked forward to its appearance with interest, and expected it long ago. I must therefore make an explanation of its delay. To secure its early issue, and having other duties to attend to, I constantly sat up burning the nightly oil long after all others around were 'hushed in nature's sweet repose,' and forwarded the manuscript to the printer in the first week of April. From previous correspondence I anticipated its readiness for publication early in May. But from incidental circumstances in his department affecting other works in his hands equally with mine, it was not commenced for some time after receipt, and its progress afterwards was protracted by intermittent cessations from press of special business. But while regretting (and fretting somewhat at) the delay, I have taken advantage of it to add some more useful matter, and among other things, in the Appendices at the end; where the reader will find specimens of the style and policy adopted in high and lower quarters of misrepresentations in connection with ourselves, and will not fail to see in them an identity in nature and aim with those on the question in general brought out to view throughout this treatise.

August, 1876.   J. B.

PREFACE.

THE first part of the following treatise is a lecture I delivered to a very large meeting in our Presbyterian Church here on the 27th of January last, on the systematic policy of misquotation from Infant Baptists of eminence in books issued by Baptist Publication Societies, circulated widely among the people, and made use of largely by Baptist ministers in their discourses; with a review of the early church History of Infant Baptism and the Baptist policy of misrepresentation on that subject; established from their own writings. The following explanation of local matters will enable the reader to understand the immediate bearing and occasion of that lecture. In June last (1875) the Baptist congregation here (which is close communionist) opened their new church, and in September following, engaged the services for some time of the Rev. Mr. Carnes to minister to them, who remained till the end of February. He at once entered on his labours with marked vigour of speech, and some striking peculiarities of doctrine and manners. His characteristic style was throughout denunciatory of other denominations. Among other things he constantly took exception to the commonly believed duty and value of prayer in relation to "forgiveness" and "salvation," to use his own expressions. To pray for these he described as useless and contrary to the New Testament. Our sins were buried more than 1800 years ago in the grave with Christ; God offers forgiveness as a gift, which we are to take, but not to ask. None ever got salvation in answer to prayer. In old times it used to be, Seek and ye shall find, but is different now; it is Jesus who seeks us. Also, to exhort unbelievers to pray to God, which he spoke of as commonly practised, he denounced (though none of the usual denominations, so far as I know, exhort any to pray in unbelief, but the reverse. We got the name of it, however). He spoke strongly against the practice of teaching children to pray the Lord's Prayer. In short, prayer according to him, ought to begin only after forgiveness has been received, which is not to be asked for itself at all, nor whatever else he meant by 'salvation.' The first day of the week he affirmed, was not the *Sabbath* day. The Word of God is the only rule of faith, and in it the Sabbath was never changed from the seventh day to the first, etc. Those acquainted with Plymouth Brethrenism will recognise the above as identical with it on those subjects: and, withal, he was a very zealous Baptist. For Infant Baptism and sprinkling, or "baby sprinkling" as, (like Baptists generally) he preferred to call it, he had all abhorrence. As he described himself from time to time, he spoke "fearlessly," without "mincing" his words. Caricature and ridicule, (for which he had a particular taste) he used without reserve.

It so happened also, as the Methodist minister and myself have congregations at a distance to attend to in the after part of each Sabbath, that there was no other evening meeting in the village, except in the Baptist church; to which from that circumstance, with the striking novelties of Mr. C.'s doctrines, laughable allusions, and his assaults on Infant Baptists in general, and Infant Baptism, a considerable number of the village people went in the evenings to see and hear the unusual minister.

About two months fully after he came here, and when his peculiar doctrines and manners were the universal conversation, I (December 5th) preached (from John iv. 10, 13, 14), on prayer in faith on the Lord Jesus in relation to "forgiveness" and "salvation;" explained that these did not lose their character as a "gift" of unmerited grace by being given in answer to prayer; showed the exercise of prayer in that connection to be the divine will, as indicated in the text, in the petition of the Lord's prayer,—" and forgive us our trespasses," and several other passages I specified from the New Testament, as in the Lord's answer to the prayer of the thief on the cross, the publican in the temple, etc., etc. Also that it was most proper and dutiful to exhort *all*, unbelievers included, to be and do right, to believe, and pray with all the heart in that spirit. I made no allusion to Baptism. This discourse was immediately taken much amiss by Mr. Carnes, and referred to as opposition to and jealousy of him and the beginning of persecution. He reiterated his views with increased vehemence: "I say, though it were with my last breath, that no man ever got salvation by praying for it. I don't say it is a sin to pray for it, but it is of no use," etc. He also bore hard on the infirmities of Infant Baptists (not of Baptists) and the great evil, "baby sprinkling."

Towards the end of the preceding winter, I had thought of the desirability, if possible, of giving a course of lectures, monthly or so, during the next, on several useful subjects (not controversial) more suitably dealt with in that way than on Sabbath, as a regular ministry having been only recently settled here for the first time, many necessarily had grown up without the advantage of such information. When last winter came round I accordingly thought of this again. At that time the subject of Confessions of Faith was being discussed by the press for some time, in connection with the case of the Rev. Mr. Macdonnell of Toronto. One of the most, or the most virulent attack on ours and our Presbyterian church, appeared on the 28th October, in the *Canadian Baptist* of Toronto, *the* Close Communionists' leading denominational weekly paper of this Province, to which my attention was drawn. Mr. Macdonnell, in a sermon to his congregation last September, gave lengthened expression to his doubts of the Scripturality of the doctrine of everlasting punishment, and stated that he considered that the Westminster Confession should have left it an open question. At the opening of Knox College, in his remarks on that occasion, he alluded to our Confession as in some things "a fetter," and hoped for its revisal and modification. Among others, the Rev. Mr. Robb of Toronto, one of the most esteemed and able ministers of our church, remarked his regret that Mr. McD. should have introduced that question on such an occasion, also that such a declaration was inconsistent with his having but a few months before accepted and declared the Westminster Confession to be the Confession of his faith, in terms of the Basis of Union. I make this explanation for the better understanding of the bearing of what follows. That attack in the *Canadian Baptist* was placed in the section of its first page permanently headed " THE BAPTIST PULPIT." I will now give you some specimens from it. Alluding to what I have explained of Mr. Robb, it says, "It is no wonder that the Rev Mr. Robb, the champion of the Confession stood up with *holy wrath* haloing his *natural dignity.*" Again, "Is not the Presbyterian Church of Canada *built on* the same Confession of faith?" "if it can be proven after all that this great wealthy and influential church be *not* built upon *the foundation of Christ and his apostles.*" etc. "The Confession is now looked upon, not only as the guide of the church in faith and practice, but *even* as an INFALLIBLE CODE of ethics and religion." What gross calumny, and how the Baptist people are prejudiced against us by untruth! It concludes thus: "So long as the church and her standards were *elevated above* the Bible, Infant Baptism had the promise of a long reign. But if the sharp, gleaming, two-edged sword of the Spirit is what is to try the doctrines and practices of the church, then it is doomed to perish. The axe which is before long to lie at the root of this ancient but rotten tree, is already sharpening on the grindstone of public opinion and soon it shall fall a huge mass of hollow rottenness." Such was the character of that unchristian emanation of antagonism. The *Canadian Baptist* has a number of subscribers here. I may remark, by the way, that the spirit and style of the above is just such as continually characterized Mr. Carnes in his animadversions.

Although I thoroughly disliked the idea of engaging in the war of words and water connected with the Baptist controversy, with which, too, experience shows they are usually sure to add any amount of virulence the more clearly that the weakness of their cause is made apparent, and there was every reason to expect such an accompaniment here, it was now evident, however, that in the faithful discharge of the sacred responsibilities of the ministerial office, and the interests of truth and true religion, such personal feelings must be refused, and direct dealing with the questions at issue would have to be engaged in, the way things were being driven by Mr. C., and on vital doctrines as well, who, as yet, had it all his own way. I may say also that my brother minister of the Methodist denomination (who has had considerable experience of Baptists in this line of things, and is of a mild disposition), when we met from time to time, expressed to me as his view that this course was necessary; but Presbyterians being the more numerous, and I being longer here, it was considered proper that I should undertake it. In the circumstances, and as few, if any, of my congregation and others here had ever heard the subject of Confessions formally explained, I decided on choosing it for my first monthly lecture, and on the same Sabbath that I preached the forementioned discourse on prayer, I intimated to my congregation my intention to give it on the 16th of December; also that I intended to criticise in connection with it, for a short time, the statements of the *Canadian Baptist* article referred to, which I described; and that, as such statements are a specimen of what is often unjustly said by Baptists and others, I intended to intimate my lecture and that intended criticism to the Baptist minister, and that he or any other Baptist minister would have an opportunity of reply in defence if they desired it. (Some B. ministers were expected to be in the village at that time at a special meeting.) I stated further that in a month or so after I thought of giving a lecture on the Early Church History of Infant Baptism, to show that Infant Baptism was not by any means an invention of the Church of Rome, as had been alleged; and, perhaps, I would give a second on that subject, as it furnished much useful instruction. This department of the subject, I may mention, I chose not only for the positive information it contains on the subject, like that of the observance of the Sabbath from the Apostles times, but also as very much bringing out to view (from Baptist books themselves) their evil spirit of misrepresentation of clearly established facts.

I accordingly sent a courteous invitation to the Baptist minister, and at the time appointed delivered my lecture on Confessions of Faith,—their Nature, Use, and Necessity,—my observations being applicable to all Confessions of any denomination. For about twenty minutes before entering on it, I read and criticised the *Canadian Baptist* article on the points just shown you from it and others. Mr. Carnes was present, and replied shortly, affirming, among other things, that the Baptists " all along, and always, had contended against Confessions of Faith." In my reply to this, I presented three *Baptist* Confessions of Faith. One drawn up by "upwards of one hundred Baptist ministers in London (England) in 1689," as itself declares, and now re-issued by Mr. Spurgeon, with a highly commendatory preface of his. That Confession being word for word literally, with scarcely a variation, except on Baptism, and *a very few* omissions, a transcript of our Westminster Confession of 1643-7. The second was "Spurgeon's Catechism," which is word for word the same as our Shorter Catechism, except on Baptism, with the omission of a few questions at the end. (These books, and another Confession, of the *Regular*

Baptist Church of Canada, which I showed next evening, I had recently purchased from the Baptist Book Room, Toronto.) And the third was a copy I *read* to the meeting of the Church Property Title Deeds of the congregations of the Regular Canada Baptist Church, including that of Chesley, *by which each congregation binds itself* to a considerable list of doctrines specified therein, and to be governed "according to the rules, regulations, and discipline of the said churches."

After I had finished these, Mr. Carnes intimated to my meeting, which was very large and a model of order throughout, that next evening in the Baptist Church my lecture of this evening and the *Canadian Baptist* article, would be reviewed. He complained that I had only read portions of the latter and not the whole (one and a quarter columns), and had dishonestly suppressed portions; but next evening it would be wholly read and my dishonesty exposed. During this meeting I made no allusion to the subject of Baptism whatever, but to Confessions alone. The next evening Mr. Carnes was chairman of his meeting, and another Baptist minister, the Rev. Peter McDonald, (who had been present at mine the evening before), was the speaker, and occupied about two and a half hours. After the meeting was opened Mr. Carnes said, without a word of explanation of the reason, then or since, that ' the *Canadian Baptist* article would be *dispensed* with, and the Rev. Mr. McDonald would address the meeting;' who began by discussing certain Greek words of the *Baptistic* controversy, and continued till I rose and reminded him that we were invited there not to a lecture on Baptism, but to hear a review of my lecture on Confessions of Faith and my alleged dishonest suppression of parts of the article in the *Canadian Baptist* exposed, and requested him to keep faith with the meeting and come to the subjects promised. He then occupied not more than twenty minutes in pointing out some statements in our Westminster Confession as in his view unscriptural, (viz.: that "faith is a saving grace," that "the first day of the week is the Sabbath," and its doctrine of election,)—a line of remark not bearing at all on the *subjects* of my lecture, (viz.: What does the expression "Confession of Faith" as applied to such documents, etc., *mean;* the different advantages of their *use;* and their *necessity* to the right working of *any* denomination of the church amid the conflicting views on the most fundamental and other important doctrines and practices that do and may exist;) he then, again, turned to Baptism on which alone he continued the rest of the evening.

There was another feature of this meeting which will never be forgotten by the hundreds who were present. When Mr. McD. (a man of middle age) began at first his manner was quiet, and I anticipated from it at least respectfulness and courtesy. But soon the disappointment was great. All through the evening his rudeness and abusiveness to myself was extreme. He did 'not care for one of my coat,' etc., etc. He shook his hand often to my face and his little book over my head, challenged me and any one of my coat to discuss with him, continually demanded answers to his many questions there and then. I said once, I will reply at the end; at which his passion only increased, and he stood putting his questions to me, demanding "Yes" or "No" with uncontrollable fierceness. Mr. Carnes, chairman though he was, never interposed a word. While he was still speaking, without indication of the end, at a quarter past nine o'clock, I rose to ask if it was intended to allow me any reply, for that the people could not be expected to wait much longer. Then when my reply came soon after, nearly every sentence I uttered was answered in retorts by Mr. McD. and Mr. Carnes, the former chiefly and sometimes both at once, Mr. McD. swaying back and fore on his chair and frequently springing to his feet as he interjected. In short it was a scene I had never seen anything approaching before, nor I presume any of the people there. I am also thankful to my God and Lord who girded me with strength that all through the provocations and trying ordeal, as all have borne witness since, Baptists also admitting the same, I was enabled not to violate in a single instance the most careful courtesy in both meetings.

Let my reader give the following its due weight. All these things I have yet narrated and will yet, are matters of public notoriety well known to hundreds here who will read these pages, which of itself is a guarantee apart from my own regard for the sacred obligation of truthfulness, of the correctness of my statements; as it would be simply suicidal to misrepresent the facts under the eyes of many—of my own congregation and others—well acquainted with them. *I have dwelt on this and the other matters the more particularly* on account of the marvellous efforts made by the other side to relieve the situation by communications to papers at a distance full of misrepresentations to outsiders, who don't know the facts.

The things brought out at these meetings, and

especially the unworthy conduct described (far short of the reality) brought the Baptist side of things into much disrepute. Mr. Carnes, however, whatever he may have felt, did not lose courage to persevere. Infant and sprinkling baptism, and prayer as not to be made for salvation, received continued and much attention. Some pamphlets on the former subject began to be issued in private. I had not accepted their challenges, of course, because I dare not. He had said in regard to my intimation mentioned, of my intended lecture on the Early Church History of Infant Baptism, that I would not give it while he was here. The time came round. Things on the other side were not improving. Baptists and others might justly think that a cause might be good although its advocates were deficient; the Baptists are also very zealous here in their views, and without doubt sincere. Under the teaching they have been subject to they are kept in ignorance of the true facts, and over zeal in matters of this kind is particularly blinding, like Pharisaism. Something positive on the subject seemed needful. The Methodist minister, like myself, was of this mind. On the 16th of January I intimated my lecture on Infant Baptism for the 27th instant. Immediately Mr. C. anticipated it by intimating discourses of his own on Baptism for the Sabbath preceding its delivery, morning and evening. I was present at the latter. It was occupied largely by his reading of many professed quotations from Infant Baptist writers in favour of immersion. After he had closed the meeting by the benediction, I requested him to oblige me with the name of the Baptist book he read those quotations from, to verify them. He said he would not give it. I otherwise ascertained it in a way my readers will learn afterwards, and in my lecture on the following Thursday evening exposed in IT a number of *thorough misquotations* by comparison with their originals. The following pages exhibit these. The first part of this treatise contains that lecture then delivered, only that my time then being very limited for the work in hand the quotations in several instances were not made so full as they otherwise would, and the reasoning on many points was necessarily brief. The same are now more extended here.

This lecture was sufficient. The meeting was very large and orderly. Mr. Carnes being present and offered an opportunity of reply, did not accept it, but gave one the week following in his own church. Like the former, in the same place on the 17th December, it was distinguished by much rudeness on his part. In matter, his recourse was chiefly to past and present persecution of Baptists by Presbyterians, but said nothing of the historical records of Ana-Baptist improprieties. I have never alluded to things of this kind. I was refused reply, however short. He also had recourse to a most extraordinary expedient of getting *Special Constables* stationed in his meeting, under the pretence that he believed there was danger of serious disturbance; of which there was not the least likelihood or intention. Having thus arranged, he spoke throughout in manner much fitted to provoke the peoples' feelings, but they bore it with admirable patience, One part of the design in this remarkable procedure seems to have been to lead Baptists and others, outside of this immediate neighbourhood, to suppose us very fierce, and to have been consciously and plainly unable to maintain our position in the controversy. In point of fact, this 'face' was put on it in a communication in a paper of Kincardine, around which Baptists are somewhat numerous; and in the *Canadian Baptist* to its readers all over the Province.

The system adopted in this cause as pushed by Close Communionists in particular, is notably much the same all over the country, and is very bad in principle, as the reader will see in these pages, and very injurious to themselves and others. As in all such cases, the great majority of them are misled and know it not. We wish them well. For the interests of truth and true religion, we have felt it our duty to make this small contribution in unfolding what would be well to be much better known. It is hoped that, by the divine blessing, this may be of some service to preserve some from the evils, and perhaps to aid a few, already involved, to a more excellent way.

I will close these prefatory remarks by some extracts from a treatise on this subject by John Bunyan, which I find in his works now before me, entitled, "Differences in Judgment about Water Baptism, No Bar to Communion." It occupies fully twenty closely printed folio pages. He thus describes its contents: "To communicate with saints, as saints, proved lawful. In answer to a book written by the Baptists," etc. He next quotes the following, with reference to those he replies to: "Should not the multitude of words be answered? And, should a man full of talk be justified? Should thy lies make men hold their peace? And when thou mockest shall no man make thee an answer?—Job xi. 2, 3. I am for peace; but when I speak they are for war.—Ps. cxx. 7." He then has a short prefatory letter "to the reader," from which I make the following extract: "All I say is that the Church of Christ hath not warrant to keep out of their communion the Christian that is discovered to be a visible saint by the word, the Christian that walketh according to his light with God. I will not make reflections upon those unhandsome brands that my brethren have laid upon me for this, as, that I am a Machiavelian, a man devilish, proud, insolent, presumptuous, and the like. Neither will I say as they, 'the Lord rebuke thee;' words fitter to be spoken to the devil than a brother. But, reader, read and compare, lay aside prejudice and judge. What Mr. Kiffin hath done in the matter, I forgive, and love him never the worse; but must stand by my principles." I will now give you a few extracts from his treatise to show the rude way in which they, *the Close Communion Baptists* of his day, assailed that prince in Israel. He begins it: "Sir, your seemingly serious reflections upon that part of my plain-hearted confession of faith, which rendereth a reason of my freedom to communicate with those of the saints and faithful who differ from me about water baptism, I have read and considered. . . . But, finding yours (if I mistake not) far short of a candid replication, I thought convenient, not only to tell you of those impertinencies everywhere scattered up and down in your book, but, also that, in my simple opinion, your rigid and church disquieting principles are not fit for any age and state of the church."

He next replies to the objections of his leading opponent, and says: "The first is that you closely disdain my person, because of my low descent among men, stigmatizing me for a person of that rank that need not be heeded or attended to." "What need you: before you have shewed one syllable of a reasonable argument in opposition to what I assert, thus trample my person, my gifts, my grace, (have I any?) so disdainfully under your feet," etc. Again, further on, "And even now, before I go any further, I will give you a touch of the reason of my publishing that part of my book which you so hotly oppose. It was because of those continual assaults that the rigid brethren of your way made, not only upon this congregation to rent it, but also upon many others about us, if peradventure they might break us in pieces, and draw from us disciples after them. Assaults, I say, upon this Congregation by times for no less than sixteen years." "Neither did they altogether fail of their purpose; for some they did rent and dismember from us." . . . "But to pass these, the wild and unsound positions they have urged to maintain their practice, would be too large here to insert." "Do but grant me without mocking of me, the liberty you desire to take, and God helping me, I desire no more to shift for myself among you." He adds, "As to your saying that I proudly and imperiously insult, because I say they are babes and carnal, that attempt to break the peace and communion of churches, though upon no better pretence than water; you must know I am still of that mind, and shall be, so long as I see the effects that follow, viz.: the breach of love, taking off Christians from the more weighty things of God, and to make them quarrel and have heartburnings one against another. Where you are pleased to charge me with raging, for laying those eighteen particular crimes to the charge of such who exclude Christians from Church Communion," etc. "Nay, you make want of light therein (on baptism) a ground to exclude the most godly from your communion, when every novice in religion shall be received unto your bosom, and be of esteem with you, because he hath (and from what grounds God knows) submitted to water baptism." These extracts are taken all from the first two pages, and are specimens of the matter of the treatise throughout. They show the spirit and modes of action of the Close Communionists in Bunyan's day, (he died in A.D. 1688), and how that eminently pious and useful minister with others were assailed and their congregations harrassed by them. Those acquainted with that body of our day, in Canada, etc., cannot fail to recognize in Bunyan's record an exact description of their spirit and manner of carrying out their great aim at present, all over, of which, also, we have just had such a lively representation among ourselves.

J. BETHUNE.

CHESLEY, ONT., *April, 1876.*

BAPTIST MISREPRESENTATIONS ON BAPTISM.

> "But unto them that do Him fear,
> God's mercy never ends;
> And to their children's children still
> His righteousness extends."—PSALM ciii. 17.

THE subject of Baptism is an interesting one to all Christians, as one of the two symbolical ordinances instituted by the Lord Jesus to be observed by his church under the New Testament dispensation. Similar in nature to the erroneous doctrine of Transubstantiation and its accompaniments, held by the church of Rome in relation to the Lord's Supper, many also regard the regeneration of the soul as effected by the baptism of water. I need not explain that we, by no means, agree with those doctrines. Baptism and the Lord's Supper have a place and value, but not in the sense nor to the extent that these imagine. In regard to Baptism, there is also a keen contention by some about the proper mode of its administration, and the proper persons to be baptized. I refer to those who are called, on this account, Baptists, their name indicating the prominence they give to these aspects of the question. Formerly the name given them was Anabaptists, the meaning of which is Rebaptizers, and which, from us, is more appropriate, considering the suitableness of meaning. For, to call them Baptists, to distinguish them from ourselves and other denominations on this subject, implies, if the signification of the word be looked to, that they are, and we are not, Baptizers; that our baptism is not worthy of the name of Baptism. Yet, assuredly, we believe the ordinance, as we administer it, to be the ordinance according to the Lord's appointment. Hence, although that denomination says that our baptism is no baptism, and baptizes in their own way any who may join their congregations, who previously had been baptized in our way, WE can only regard such as baptized over again, and those who practice it as *Rebaptizers*. Although, *perhaps*, it is not worth our while contending about the name, since it is employed apart from its own meaning, like proper names of persons, merely to designate the denomination referred to, still it implies in its meaning what that denomination contends for as true of themselves alone, and what we refuse to admit as correct in reality. And, as in the case of Romanists, in regard to the name "Catholic," it may be better to form the habit of giving them the proper appellation. It would be too much, certainly, for them to expect or require from us that we call them Baptists and ourselves not, when we do regard them as Rebaptizers, and ourselves as Baptists. I will not, however, myself alter the name to-night.

In our opinion, the Baptists go far to excess on this question. Experience shows us it is quite possible to go to improper extremes in this as in other things, and in many ways, as the Scribes and Pharisees did on the Scripture ordinance of the Sabbath, etc.; and many do, as before stated as to Transubstantiation and Baptismal Regeneration. While we don't wish to under-appreciate any Scripture truth or ordinance, it is still true to say that all things equally Scriptural are by no means of equal value. Hence a real error in regard to some may not be so serious as an error in others. For instance, error on baptism, say as to its administration of water, such as would nullify or abolish it (as with the Quakers for example), though it would be an important error undoubtedly, yet would not be so serious in nature and consequences as the abolition of the Sabbath day, the removal from it of the obligations of the fourth commandment, or the vitiation or removal of the doctrine of salvation by faith in Christ, or of the baptism and work of the Holy Spirit.

But our Baptist brethren say they don't attach so much value to baptism as is said of them, but rather to the duty of obedience to the commandment of the Lord. This reason, they feel, is a sufficient justification of all their zeal. As to this, however, I may remark, even with such a reason, many err in many things. The Jews pleaded the fourth commandment and the other precepts of Moses against the Saviour and his disciples as to the Sabbath, whom they regarded as loose and disobedient, and were moved against Him for this, even to frenzy; and looking at the Scripture, it would not be difficult for them to make out a seemingly plausible case to the body of the people. Yet, I may ask, why this amount of zeal for the command as to baptism, more than many other commandments, if baptism itself be admitted of subordinate value? Their form of church government—Independency—they maintain is the Scripture required form, and the Presbyterian, and all others, quite wrong. Now, church government *is* an important matter, and has corresponding results. Why, then, do the Baptists not as much insist in their books, and sermons, and conversations on the Lord's will on this? But you don't hear them do so. Again, they constantly affirm in their contentions on Baptism that we ought not to teach or practise in the church anything we don't find express precept or example for in the New Testament. Well, do they carefully carry out this principle in other matters? There is the practice of instrumental music in God's house and worship. Last summer, when their church was opened here, they not only used it with the singing in each of their three Sabbath services, but even while the collections were taken up. Yes, and even 'played the people out' on their leaving church, the same as is done in theatres; a new thing as yet to other denominations in this part of the world! Long may it be so! But that is to be called the WORSHIP OF GOD!—the worship of the NEW TESTAMENT, taught and practised by the Apostles! Yet is it certainly much easier to find passages in the New Testament teaching and exemplifying our views of baptism than for them to point out there any in doctrine, precept or example, authorizing the use of instrumental music in God's House. Nor do they profess to find any there. Nor is it an unimportant matter. How, then, can they quietly adopt and use it, and not, rather, place themselves in opposition to it, since there is no trace of it in the New Testament church under the Apostles? It can be no justification for them to say that other denominations practise it as well; as they don't accept that reason for baptizing as the others do. We are afraid, though contrary to the principle they contend for in the matter of baptism, that it is favoured because a useful means in the cause of proselytism.

The Baptist doctrine that they attach only a subordinate value to the ordinance as compared with more vital things is agreeable to the ear, but how do they—especially the 'Close Communionists'—work this theory in practice? It seems plain, from their constant, eager, and in the case of a very large proportion of them, even their fanatical zeal in pushing this question always and everywhere, IN PRIVATE and in public, in conversation, books, religious papers, and church discourses, that PRACTICALLY they make it a chief thing—one of the most important. Instead of exerting their efforts in PRIVATE principally towards the conversion of souls, it is baptism, baptism, eagerly with every one they can find access to,—or 'fasten upon,' to express it more precisely; while in public they show a similar feverish zeal, though this is modified in manner of expression where other ministries prevail, but sometimes not. If they don't succeed in making proselytes, they appear to feel as though they have done nothing, and when they do succeed in this, in any case their joy, and their expression of it, is great.

In order to bring out how much value they really attach to baptism above other decidedly more important things, I will specify a striking exemplification among ourselves at this presesent time. There is the Baptist minister, who has been ministering to the congregation in Chesley for the past five months or so. He has been often and designedly preaching against 'prayer for salvation'—to use his own mode of expression,—which is a very important matter indeed, much more so than baptism. He has frequently said that no one ever got salvation by praying for it; that he would not give that, viz.: the crack of his finger and thumb, for prayer offered for salvation; and such like sayings. He has also maintained that the *first* day of the week is not the Sabbath day, and it follows, of course, that the fourth commandment could not then apply to it to keep it free from secular occupations; and he has other seriously erroneous Plymouth doctrines. Moreover, he has been in the CONSTANT HABIT of cracking JOKES to his audiences IN CHURCH ON SABBATH, disposing them to LAUGHTER, and sometimes to laugh right out; with other expedients for gathering meetings. Just fancy me, brethren, cracking jokes in my pulpit on Sabbaths—what would you who belong to my congregation think of it and say? I think I see before me your displeasure and indignation. And all honour to you for that,—you would be very right. You would not be willing to tolerate it. Or, suppose a man, after gathering his household together for family worship on any day, as well as the Sabbath, were, during the time of that worship, to mix it up with laughable stories, and similar slang remarks, would that not be grossly improper? And is not the worship of God, in God's House, on the Sabbath day, in a large meeting, and presided over by a minister, to be as solemnly and reverently conducted throughout as at home in the family? I ask, is it so, or is it not? Does it cease to be profaned if, in a church, on the Sabbath, a *minister*, in conducting it, indulges in what is laughable, by the way? Joking, and habitually so in the worship of God! Such conduct, brethren has deeply pained my heart, as most dishonouring to God and injurious to those who are under its influence. I must speak out. I cannot refrain,—in God's name, for His honour, and for the sake of the people of this place, I protest against it! Mr. Carnes, I believe, has done more to demoralize this village in religious things, during his short time, than has been done since it was a village! "God is greatly to be feared in the assembly of the saints, and to be had in reverence of all them that are about Him" (Ps. lxxxix. 7). "Ye are the salt of the earth: but if the salt have lost his savour wherewith shall it be salted?"

Now, here is the point I wish to draw your attention to. Notwithstanding that unseemly manner in divine things and those seriously erroneous doctrines, quite different from what that congregation were hitherto understood to acknowledge, still they have put up with all quietly, without a murmur. And why? Because Mr. Carnes is withal after their heart in regard to baptism, and very zealous in that connection; while the other things being singular and amusing bring out a number on whom that zeal may operate. I say, because of that. For, were he even with no objectionableness in the other matters mentioned—were he to have changed his views on that subject,—to suppose the case—and to have preached on one of those days against immersion, and in favour of infant baptism, or only one of these, who, that knows their feelings on that subject, would not be certain they would not have allowed him the opportunity of doing so a second time? We may be sure an outcry, strong and decisive, would at once be raised.

Now, it is the like of these things that test and bring out to discerning eyes the real comparative value people attach to things, and not the theoretical profession apart from the practice. The Roman Catholics tell us they don't worship their images, but regard them only as memorials of the Saviour and the other persons they represent, and use them only to assist in recalling to mind the persons represented; and that when they bow before them they mean only to honour those persons whose images they are. Such is the theory in defence, and looks plausible, at least to Romanists. But how do they work the thing? They do, *in fact*, make idols of those images, and are eager idolaters. Just the same defence the more learned among the heathen gave when the early Christians charged them with worshipping their images. "No," said they, "the celestial regions of Olympus (or elsewhere, as the case might be,) are the abode of our gods. Their images are only memorials, remembrancers. We honour not the wooden, stone, silver, or golden statues, but the gods through them." Yes, that was also their theory, but how did it work among them? They made idols of the statues; that was the sinful fact.

Now, don't let any suppose for a moment that we compare our Baptist brethren in their doctrines, faith, and manner of life generally, to Romish or heathen idolaters. No; by no means. Some of them we sincerely recognize and love as true and exemplary Christians, and many, we do not doubt, are such, though, like others, they have, of course, their infirmities, and, like other denominations, are a mixed multitude. But we have been showing by those illustrations, in point, that theory and profession are one thing, but the real nature and tendency is to be seen in the prominence given and the result produced in the practical working. Whatever Baptists may *say* as to their not regarding the ordinance of Baptism rightly administered as itself saving, but subordinate as an external symbolical rite, yet they are so spoken to by their teachers, constantly impressed and stirred up by word and books, and speak of it, and act in such a way that with *very many* of them it seems to absorb their interest, and excite their zeal for proselytism to an extent that nothing else religious does. I mean the *Close Communionists* in particular.

REASON OF MY LECTURE ON THE EARLY CHURCH HISTORY OF INFANT BAPTISM.

It has been stated by the Baptist minister in the Baptist church that infant baptism is A RELIC OF POPERY; and we all know this to be a frequent statement of Baptist ministers, publications, and people. Now, if this charge is to be inquired into, we must search into the HISTORY *of the subject.* This I have proposed to do to-night, and to show you that this charge, like many others, is a genuine misrepresentation. It is usually admitted that Popery, properly so-called, raised its head as such not till *after the first five centuries.* (Of course the principles of Popery, which are just those of fallen human nature, began to operate at the fall of man. But what is meant, and usually understood by that expression is the Romish Church in the dominance and claim of its Bishop as universal Bishop and Vicar of Christ.) This Protestants contend affirmatively against Rome. And even at the end of the sixth century, (about A.D. 597) Gregory, Bishop of Rome, wrote against the assumption of the Bishop of Constantinople, "Whosoever may claim the title of universal Bishop is the forerunner of Antichrist,"—which shows he did not himself claim that title.

The history of the church, properly authenticated is, of course, of some service like other history. For instance in regard to the *first* day of the week being the Christian *Sabbath*, if it can be undoubtedly shown from history that the Christian church sacredly observed that day as such, from the time of the Apostles, that will *aid* us in understanding the force of those passages of the New Testament which refer to it. The same will be true of Infant Baptism.

And if we can show undoubtedly that the Baptism of Infants was the practice of the church long before the time of popery, it follows that Infant Baptism is not, as charged by the Baptists, a relic of popery. But, notwithstanding, while church history has some value we do not regard or use it to *decide* for us matters of religious faith and worship.

Our only and infallible rule of faith and manners is the *Word of God*, as is expressed in our Westminster Confession of Faith, Chap. I., Sec. 6, 10 : " The whole counsel of God, concerning all things necessary for His own glory, man's salvation, faith and life, is either expressly set down in Scripture, or by good and necessary consequence may be deduced from Scripture, unto which nothing at any time is to be added, whether by revelations of the spirit, or traditions of men." " The Supreme Judge, by which all controversies of religion are to be determined, and all decrees of Councils, opinions of ancient writers, doctrines of men, and private spirits are to be examined, and in whose sentence we are to rest, can be no other but the Holy Spirit speaking in the Scripture." This, brethren, I need not tell you, is our belief and doctrine, and hence when I preach to my people I *establish* what I say always by the Word of God. But if for any purpose we wish to know the practice or events of the church of any period after the completion of the Scripture and the days of the Apostles, it is manifest we cannot ascertain *these* by the Scripture, but by the trustworthy uninspired history of those times. Consequently in my lecture to-night on the " Early Church History of Infant Baptism after the Apostolic age, and during the 2nd, 3rd, 4th and 5th centuries," we must consult, as far as available, the records on the subject that remain to us of those times.

But before entering on this question I have another line of work before me I did not know of when I intimated this lecture two weeks ago. This has been induced by discourses on Baptism by the Baptist minister in the Baptist church last Sabbath, and will give me now double work and take longer. But this line of work I must take up to-night, and in the first place, as the Baptist minister, I understand, is to leave next week for another land.

On Sabbath evening he read from a Baptist book many

quotations, said to be from eminent Infant baptist writers mentioned, and favouring Baptist views. (The word PAEDO-BAPTIST you will understand, means Infant-baptist.) This subject of such quotations I mean to throw some light upon, which cannot fail to be interesting. I may state preliminarily that at the close of that meeting, and after the blessing was pronounced, being present, I went forward and asked him if he would give me the name of the book from which he had read those quotations, and he refused to give it to me.

Now, brethren, I regard this as decidedly unfair. See what it involves. . How would it be possible for me or any of his audience to note down every word of his quotations correctly and the places in the book referred to, as quickly as he read one quotation after another out of that one book in his hand ? and he read a great many. To do so and to mark down the places and names of the works quoted from, must be done most exactly to be of any value in finding out the originals and comparing with them. All that can be done is just to put down a few words of one's own, indicating to one's self the nature of the quotations given. But supposing the originals examined, and a misquotation apparent, it would be impossible afterwards to establish it from such notes. It could be said, these were not the words as read; and you might be charged with misrepresentation without the power of defending yourself, if you have not a copy to point to of the book from which the quotation had been read. Yes, and the same thing you would certainly be liable to even if you were a short-hand writer, which few are, and noted down every word. It might be said, you put down what *you* thought proper, you did not note correctly, and you have no proof of correctness if the party will not give you the name of the book containing the words of quotation. (Moreover, few can read shorthand besides the writer himself). Now all this can be at once and entirely avoided by the name of that book being given you. There you have the professed quotations and can with them examine the originals they are said to be taken from, and if any be incorrect you can bring the originals and make the error manifest, so that none can gainsay it. It is, therefore, a necessity and a right in the protection and promotion of truth and character. Surely this is plain to every one. Besides, if a man is conscious he has honest quotations, is it not his wisdom as well as duty to others at once to afford every facility for thorough investigation? Truth and honesty come to the light and court inspection. The Baptist minister refused me on Sabbath evening, and this is not the only case. Many of you were present at the meeting in the Baptist church, on the 17th December, when another Baptist minister, having undertaken to review my lecture delivered here on Confessions of Faith the night before, gave a lecture *instead* on BAPTISM, contrary to promise and the terms of intimation and although I had made no remarks whatever on the subject of Baptism at my meeting; *he* also quoted from a small book, passage after passage, of professed quotations from Paedobaptist writings. I *twice* asked him during the evening to oblige me with the name of the book he was reading them from, but each time he said, "O I can do that," yet would not give it, but went on with his lecture.

But the present Baptist minister, Mr. Carnes, I am glad to see is with us to-night. The reason he gave me last Sabbath for refusing the name of the book was the unsuitableness of the day, and that he did not want any discussion. I told him I intended no discussion and wished only the name of the book. Still he refused it, referring me to the Paedobaptist works he had mentioned, to go there. Well, this is Thursday, and that objection cannot hold now. I therefore ask you, now, Mr. Carnes, [who sat opposite the lecturer on the front seat] if you will give me the name of that book. I wish to have it for the purpose of verifying those quotations to see if they are correct? [Rev. Mr. Carnes kept silent. Again the lecturer proceeded]. Mr. Carnes does not answer me; he refuses still. I ask you once more, Mr. Carnes, in the presence of this large meeting, to inform me of the name of that Baptist book you read those professed quotations from Paedobaptist writers from. I and all the Paedobaptists here have a right to receive it from you. You have no right to withhold it. [Mr. Carnes, thus appealed to, said from his seat he was not prepared to grant the request; and the lecturer said] You have heard his refusal, and it is not Sabbath night; he cannot make that the excuse. I maintain that this is most unjust to us. But though it were Sabbath night ; surely if it were a proper thing to *read* the quotations on the Sabbath, it would be just as proper to have given the name of the book containing them, which he ought to have done before reading them, without being asked. And if no impropriety in reading from that book, where could be the impopriety in my respectfully asking its name after his meeting was over, since he did not give it himself, and in his giving it to me then ? The two things were of the same nature. No, brethren, the real reason is something else. I will throw some light on that yet. But I am happy to be able to say I *know the book, and I have it here on the table.* Mr. Carnes, I am sure, will recognize its name when I tell him it is "Pengilly's Scripture Guide to Baptism." I had been looking over it a short time before, and I recognized it as his while Mr. Carnes was reading. I also took down each passage of Scripture read, and quotation, in my note book, and at home compared them and found them identical and in the same order and comments. It was "Pengilly." I will shew you some things in it to-night.

I have now two things to do.

I. To show you by convincing evidence that Baptists in their zeal for propagating their opinions on baptism and in proselytising, deal very freely in misrepresentation and violations of the ninth commandment—" Thou shalt not bear FALSE witness against thy neighbour."

II. The Early Church History of Infant Baptism.

In treating the second of these subjects, the first will be seen to pervade it; yet we can enter on the first for a while by itself. And here I wish to say that I will give out the titles of the various books I read and quote from, which are all on the table before me. I also invite the Baptist minister to sit beside me—or any other—to examine the books, and overlook my reading ; moreover, if any wish to examine them in private afterwards, and call on me, I will lend them for the purpose if only I am guaranteed their safe return.

I. I now enter on my first division, viz. : Baptist misrepresentations, misquotations, &c.

The first work I will read from is the "Baptist History by Dr. Cramp, Professor of Acadia (Baptist) College, Nova Scotia ; Edition, 1875." I may say I purchased it and the other Baptist books I will use from the Baptist Book Room, Toronto. Dr. Cramp stands very high in his denomination. To do him and you justice, brethren, (as you will receive opportunities of seeing the merits otherwise) I will read you one or two commendations of him from high Baptist authorities: In the "Introductory Notice" of this edition of his "Baptist History," the writer of it, who is Dr. Angus, Professor of Baptist College, Regent's Park, London, Eng., says of Dr. Cramp, "His candour and intelligence, his love of good men, and appreciation of great principles, have won the esteem and affection of all who know him. These qualities will be found to distinguish this volume. The reader will find a fuller and more satisfactory account in these pages than anywhere besides," etc. Dr. Geo. B. Taylor (an eminent American Baptist), is the author of this small book in my hand, issued by the Baptist Publication Society, and entitled "The Baptists: Who they are, and what they have done." In it he says (p. 22), "I prefer to rely on Cramp, who, claiming less, is much more to be relied on for what he does claim. I repeat that I have been greatly impressed with his soberness, impartiality, and truthfulness, as a historian." So much, then, for the standing among Baptists of Dr. Cramp's Baptist History.

1. I will now read from it on RICHARD BAXTER, *Presbyterian.* In page 269 he calls him "the great Richard Baxter." Speaking of him again, in page 275, he says, "There was a wonderful outcry AGAINST *immersion.* Even BAXTER allowed himself to use expressions which might be laughed at, were it not for the melancholy fact that in his case (for he could not be ignorant on the subject) prejudice and passion prevailed over Christian charity, and impelled him to adopt a course which, in his sober moments, he must have condemned. Take a specimen or two :—' That which' (This is now, you observe, a quotation by Cramp from Baxter's writings) ' That which is a plain breach of the sixth commandment, *Thou shalt not kill,* is NO ORDINANCE OF GOD, but a *most heinous sin.* But the ordinary practice of BAPTIZING OVER HEAD, and in cold water as necessary, is A PLAIN BREACH of the sixth commandment; therefore, IT IS NO *ordinance of God,* BUT A HEINOUS SIN, and, as Mr. Craddock shows in his book of Gospel liberty, the

magistrate ought to restrain it, to save the lives of his subjects. In a word, it is good for nothing but to despatch men out of the world that are burdensome, and to ranken churchyards. I conclude, if murder be a sin, then DIPPING ordinarily OVER HEAD in England IS A SIN; and if those who make it men's religion to murder themselves, and urge it upon their consciences as their duty, are not to be suffered in a commonwealth any more than highway murderers; then judge how these Anabaptists, that teach the necessity of such dipping, are to be suffered." Now, the question is not whether Baxter's views, here quoted by Cramp, were right or wrong, but *what were* his views on immersion, Cramp himself being the witness. It is plain enough he held it as "*no ordinance of God*, but a *heinous sin*," and that *he* did not baptize in that manner, nor countenance it in others.

But let us now hear the same writer, on the same Baxter in another book of his, called "A Catechism on Baptism, by J. M. Cramp, D.D." In its preface he dates it "Acadia College, 1865." In page 43 he gives several professed quotations from eminent Paedobaptists to show that they FAVOURED baptism by immersion. Among them is the following as from "RICHARD BAXTER, *Presbyterian*":—"In OUR baptism WE ARE DIPPED under the water, as signifying OUR covenant profession, that as he was buried for sin, so we are dead and buried to sin." These are given as the words of THE SAME Baxter. The contradictoriness of these two quotations is very plain, and it is to be observed that Cramp gives NO INDICATION of the volume or place in all the many works of Baxter in which this last quotation may be seen. Recollect, too, that these are not merely two different Baptist books I have quoted from, which would look bad enough, but both are by the same Dr. Cramp, Baptist College Professor. It may be added that the Catechism which makes Baxter such a favourer of immersion is a small cheap book, paper covers, for wide circulation among the common people; while the other is large and less likely to be purchased by them. In the latter quotation, Baxter is represented as saying, "In OUR baptism WE are dipped,' &c., which would lead the believing reader to suppose that he and his fellow Presbyterians generally were baptized themselves as well as baptizers in that mode. Certainly if a Baptist should say, "In *our* baptism we are dipped," he would be understood to mean himself and his denomination. And yet who that knows the facts but knows that that was not true of Presbyterians, Cramp himself being witness to Baxter and them as shown in the former quotation. The unlearned Baptists and others, however—and they are of course very numerous all over—may be, and no doubt are, led by such statements as this to believe the opposite, while Presbyterians may be expected to attach great weight to such a statement as from Baxter. And all the more of course will they do so when they read the high commendations of him who misleads them, as distinguished for "soberness, impartiality, and truthfulness." We will see further into this presently. Here then there is an evident misquotation.

2. The next instance I draw your attention to is connected with the great JOHN WESLEY. I will read you a professed quotation from him in "Pengilly's Scripture Guide to Baptism," which is the Baptist book, out of which the Baptist minister here read the many professed quotations from Paedobaptist writers last Sabbath, and the name of which he three different times refused to tell me. In page 47 is the following in favour of immersion, from— "MR. JOHN WESLEY, '*Buried with him*, alluding to the ancient manner of baptizing by immersion.' Note on Rom. vi. 4." These are given as John Wesley's words. No more is added, but just as now quoted. The impression produced, and no doubt intended to be produced, on the unsuspecting reader is that these represent the view on immersion of Wesley, the great Methodist preacher and leader, as the only mode of baptism in the apostles' days. Yet the facts are not so. His many works are long before the Christian world, in one of which he expressed his views at length on this subject, which leaves misrepresentation of them the more inexcusable. I will now give you from it what he says on Rom. vi. 4, and the question generally from this "Catechism of Baptism," in my hand, of the Rev. Dr. Currie, enlarged edition, 1874, Methodist Book Room, Toronto." Dr. Currie says, p. 57, "Mr. Wesley published a TREATISE on Baptism in Nov. 1756 (Works, vol. vi., p. 12). He says (in that treatise), 'Concerning baptism,

INFANT BAPTISM.   15

I shall inquire what it is. . . . It was instituted in the room of circumcision. It CANNOT be certainly proved from Scripture that even John's baptism was performed BY DIPPING, . . . nor the Saviour's, nor that by the disciples. No; nor that of the eunuch by Philip. And as nothing can be determined from Scripture precept or example, so neither from the force or meaning of the word. For the words *baptize* and *baptism* do not necessarily imply dipping, but ARE used in OTHER senses in several places. Thus we read that the Jews 'were all baptized in the cloud and in the sea' (1 Cor. x. 2), but they were not plunged in either. They could therefore be only sprinkled by drops of the sea water and refreshing dews from the clouds.' [Wesley next specifies Christ's and his two disciples' baptism of blood (Mark x. 38), as a washing or sprinkling with it, not a dipping; and similarly of the Pharisees' washing of pots, cups, and tables or beds, of which, he remarks, " the outsides of them only were washed "—the cup and the platter (Matt. xxiii. 25), &c., and then continues. AND MARK THIS that follows, as it is on Rom. vi. 4, and Coloss. ii. 12, the texts on which Pengilly &c., represent him as an immersionist. He says:] 'It is true we read of being buried with Christ in baptism, but NOTHING can be inferred from such a figurative expression. Nay, if it held exactly it would make as much for sprinkling as for plunging; since in burying, the body is not plunged through the substance of the earth, but rather earth is poured or sprinkled upon it. And as there is no clear proof of dipping in Scripture, so there is very probable proof of the contrary. It is highly probable the apostles themselves baptized great numbers, not by dipping, but by washing, sprinkling, or pouring water. This clearly represented the cleansing from sin, which is figured by baptism. And the quantity of water used was not material; no more than the quantity of bread and wine in the Lord's Supper.'" He then refers to the baptisms of the Jailer, and Cornelius, and their households, and that of the 3,000 on the day of Pentecost, &c., as against the immersion theory. Such, brethren, were the published views and practice of Wesley, before Pengilly, Cramp, &c., were born, and yet with all that evidence before their eyes, they are as silent on it to their readers as the grave; but one and another, and yet again others, represent him as teaching that the baptisms of Scripture WERE by immersion! Let me add another instance about him: "Dr. Cramp says," (correspondence *Christian Messenger*, Feb. 22nd, 1865), "He," (Stewart) 'asks for one instance of dipping. Let him read the New Testament. Every record of baptism in that book is an instance of dipping, AS John Wesley and ministers of all Christian denominations *have* AGAIN and AGAIN *confessed.*'" (Currie's Cat. p. 55.) Here Cramp affirms Wesley to have taught that EVERY baptism recorded in the New Testament *was* administered by that mode! But when we look into his own work on the subject, as in the extracts I have just given you, and remember too, that he (and the Methodist Church) habitually administered it by sprinkling, what can we think of such a style of baptist advocacy and treatment of opponents!

4. The next misrepresentation I will show you is of Dr. A. CLARKE, another eminent Methodist.

In Cramp's Catechism on Baptism (p. 43) is the following as from him: "DR. ADAM CLARKE, *Wesleyan.* 'It is probable that the apostle here (in Rom. vi. 4) alludes to the mode of administering baptism by immersion, the whole body being put under the water.'" This is all Cramp's quotation, from which it is hoped, of course, that his readers will conclude that Clarke believed in immersion as the Scriptural and Apostolic mode. But—but the question remains for us to ask and to answer, for Cramp gives no hint of any deficiency—is this a fair quotation? In answer I will now read you from "Currie's Catechism of Baptism," (p. 54). He remarks: "Dr. Cramp quotes (Catechism p .40) from Dr. A. Clarke's Notes on Rom. vi. 4: [Currie repeats the words *verbatim* as I have read them to you from Cramp, and then proceeds] Dr. Clarke ADDS an *important qualification* to the above passage which Dr. Cramp carefully omits, (namely,) 'I say it is *probable* that the apostle alludes to this mode of immersion; but it is not absolutely *certain* that he does so, as some do imagine; for in the NEXT VERSE our being incorporated into Christ by *baptism* is also denoted by our being *planted*, or rather *grafted together in the likeness of his death;* and Noah's ark *floating* upon the water, and *sprinkled by the rain from heaven,* IS *a figure* CORRESPONDING TO *baptism.*'" [Since quoting this from Currie, I got Clarke's own works from a friend and find it *verbatim* as here given.] Now here, brethren, is the true representation of what Dr. Clarke did say on that passage. And why did not Dr. Cramp complete the quotation thus far? He could not but see it, of course. Why, but because he did not wish Dr. Clarke's REAL sentiments to be seen, while he professes to represent them correctly.

It seems Dr. Broaddus (Baptist) adopted the same plan of quotation from Dr. Clarke (and many other Baptists do so we may presume), to which Slicer, in his Work on Baptism, fifth edition, replies, page 108, "Mr. Broaddus in his Strictures, page 15, after quoting *part of a sentence* from Dr. Clarke's Commentary on Rom. vi. 4, says: 'I do think I have proved, beyond all question, that *baptizo* means to immerse, *and nothing else.* It has but one meaning—these learned men knew it (Dr. Clarke, &c.), and *their candour forced* them to *acknowledge* it'"—that is, that it means "to immerse *and nothing else.*" Now let any one consider what Dr. Clarke did say, as I have quoted in full, and not Drs. Broaddus' and Cramp's garbled misrepresentations of it, and what will he think of such statements and tactics.

5. On the GREEK CHURCH's mode of baptism, I will read first from "Pengilly's Guide to Scripture Baptism," p. 72, a quotation by him from a *Baptist* writer, viz., "Mr. R. Robinson. 'The native Greeks must understand their own language better than foreigners, and they have ALWAYS understood the word baptism to signify dipping; and therefore from their first embracing of Christianity, to this day, *they have always* baptized, and do yet baptize, by *immersion.* This is an authority for the meaning of the word infinitely preferable to that of European lexicographers. In this case the Greeks are unexceptionable guides.' *Hist. of Bapt.*, pp. 5,6." Mr. Robinson has no hesitation, no want of decidedness, in the above affirmations, and Pengilly repeats them in his book as trustworthy. The point remains, are these things really so?

But let us also hear Dr. Cramp. In his Catechism, page 48, he asks: "Has the Greek Church EVER sustained sprinkling or pouring?" And he answers, "No. I was about to say that this is remarkable. But it is not remarkable. The New Testament was written in Greek. In speaking of baptism the apostles used the Greek word *baptizo*. Christians now-a-days differ about the meaning of that word. What can be fairer than to submit the question to the Greeks themselves? They must surely understand their own language. Now, the Greeks have ALWAYS held baptism to be immersion, and they have practised accordingly. They do so to this day, even during the severity of a RUSSIAN winter. The Russians, you are aware, belong to the Greek Church."

These affirmations, brethren, you observe are decided and without any hesitation. Their readers will of course consider they must KNOW what they say to be as they say, and that none dispute it. Now, however, let me place before you real evidence.

The first I will read from is an eminent BAPTIST, even the same Dr. Broaddus Mr. Slicer mentions in his Work on Baptism, only he was *Mr.* not Dr. then. In his small work now before me, entitled " Immersion Essential to Christian Baptism, Philadelphia: Bible and Publication Society," he gives on pages 18-19 an account in his (Broaddus's) own words, of some statements an eminent modern writer made on this subject, namely Dr. Dollinger, now famous as the leader of the Old Catholic Party in Germany, who refused to accept the Vatican Dogma of Papal Infallibility in 1870. Dr. Broaddus explains him as saying of the Greek patriarchs of the 14th century, as follows: that " a Council of them agreed, not that they would practise pouring or sprinkling, but that they would recognize it in the Westerns as valid baptism. They were almost ruined, in danger of being utterly swallowed up by the conquering Turks, and wanted to make friends with the Latin Christians. But at a later period, the Greek patriarchs retracted this. IT IS STILL OBSERVED IN RUSSIA, but those to whom Greek was the native language could not stand it," &c. Now you observe these words I have put in capitals. You remember what I just quoted you from Cramp, who affirmed without any hesitation: " They do so (baptize by immersion) to this day, even during the severity of a RUSSIAN winter. The Russians belong to the Greek church." Yet here is Broaddus stating the contrary, on the authority of Dollinger, that the same Russians administer it by "pouring or sprinkling!" That portion he gives of Dollinger's testimony we may be sure the latter did say, as certainly Broaddus would not put it in his lips otherwise; as to the other statements, seeing he does not give us Dollinger's own words, and learning by experience, we had better not accept his account of things. I will show you now that his last sentence is untrue, by the way.

Next let me read you from Currie's Catechism (page 94-96); he asks, "What does Dr. Cramp assert concerning the Greek church;" (Here Currie gives in answer the same words I quoted you myself from Cramp's Catechism, and then asks), "Are Dr. Cramp's assertions true? Dr. Cramp gives part of the truth, and suppresses part, when he says the Greek church immerses and 'does not sustain sprinkling or pouring.' Booth (a leading Baptist writer), whose work Dr. Cramp recommends, in his *Paedobaptism Examined*, quotes DEYLINGIUS as follows: 'So long as the apostles lived, *as many believe*, immersion only was used, to which afterwards, perhaps, THEY added a kind of *affusion* (that is, sprinkling or pouring) SUCH AS THE GREEKS practise AT THIS DAY, after having performed the trine immersion.'"

Currie next shows instances of the practice, as follows: "HUBER says: 'I resided upwards of THREE YEARS in the Capital of the Grand Seignior's dominions, in a GREEK family of the first respectability. During that time I was present at FOUR BAPTISMS—two in the family and two in the immediate neighbourhood. It is the custom among the Greeks either to have their children baptized publicly in their churches, or else in their houses, in which latter case the parents invite their nearest relations and neighbours; and after the ceremony, while refreshments pass round, the father gives to each person present a token of witness-ship, consisting of a small piece of Turkish money, through which a hole is pierced and a piece of new ribbon inserted. I was thus invited to attend the four above-mentioned baptisms, and I still have in my possession two tokens; the other two may be seen in Mrs. McDowall's museum in Danville. The company were all seated on the sofas around the room. A table stood in the middle, with a basin of water on it. The priest was then sent for; who, upon entering the room, was received by the father of the infant and led to the baptismal water, which he consecrated by a short prayer and the sign of a cross. Then the mother presented to him her babe, which he laid on his left arm, and in the name of the Father, Son, and Holy Ghost, he thrice dipped HIS HAND in the water and DROPPED SOME OF IT ON the child's forehead, giving it a name. . . . Most generally the infants are baptized in the churches. Before the altar stands a tripod holding a BASIN of consecrated water for baptism.' This was the baptism proper. The preparatory immersions which the Greeks—at least in some places—practise would be performed in another apartment and without the presence of the priest."

How very different an account, brethren, of the practice of the Greek church on this subject are these statements of Deylingius and Huber (with Broaddus) from those of Cramp, and Robinson, and Pengilly. The latter affirms without a sign of wincing that that church does not, and never did, baptize by sprinkling or pouring. Yet see what *Huber*, an eye-witness, has narrated of each of the four baptisms he was present at. It was by sprinkling in EACH case. He tells us also of the churches having before the altar a BASIN of consecrated water for baptism; and a *basin* is evidently not intended for immersing persons in, but to sprinkle from. *Deylingius* asserts distinctly that *affusion* or sprinkling is the mode " such as the Greeks practice at this day," and indicates that this mode was practised all through the ages. Of immersion he says :— " Many *believe* " (that is, many of the Greek church) that it alone was used while the apostles lived; which implies that they (the same persons) believed otherwise of the times from immediately after the apostles; and also that *many others believe* immersion was not the only mode, or the mode at all, in the apostles' time. But these opinions are not the question. Many of the Greek church no doubt believe that their worship of the Virgin Mary and images was also practised in the apostles' days. We see from Huber and Deylingius that the Greek church instead of not practising sprinkling now or ever, really do and have throughout the past been doing this very thing. And observe that the above quotation of Deylingius is taken from *Booth's Paedobaptist Examined*, a Baptist writer of high standing among them, and a book stored with materials to use by other Baptist writers as they see fit—with which Dr. Cramp is well acquainted, and from which he quotes. Pengilly also in his " Scripture Guide to Baptism "—the same I have been reading from to-night—of 86 pages, makes about 40 from it of professed quotations from Paedobaptist writers. [And here I will pause a moment to show you by the way the value others who have examined it have come to ascribe to this work of *Booth*. And preliminarily let me notify what Pengilly states in a note at the bottom of page 71 of his "Guide to Baptism," viz., " See this author (Calvin) and those that follow cited at greater length and their work referred to in Booth's 'Paedobaptist Examined,' Vol. 1. pp. 44 to 65, EIGHTY-TWO such authorities are there adduced." Slicer on Baptism says, page 114: " Now, candid reader, I leave you to judge how much reliance is to be placed on the mutilated testimonies from Paedobaptist writers adduced by Mr. Broaddus. You can judge of the balance from those I have examined. I will close this part of the subject with a quotation from that clear and conclusive writer, Peter Edwards, who was himself for a number of years a Baptist preacher, and who discovered the weakness of the arguments of the Baptists while reading Mr. BOOTH's *book* in favour of their views. He says (speaking of Mr. Booth's eighty witnesses, to which Mr. Broaddus refers), ' He (Booth) quotes a number of authors, who, *as he says*, understood the term baptize to mean immersion, POURING, AND SPRINKLING ; and these quotations he calls concessions. Concessions of what ? That the word meant immersion ONLY ? If so, he made them concede what they never did concede, and what they had no thought of conceding. It is a shame to abuse the living or the dead, and it is a bad cause that requires it ; I doubt whether ONE of the EIGHTY abused critics was on his side.' Edwards, pp. 159 and 160." Thus far from the Baptist minister, Edwards, who lost faith in the Baptist cause from reading this BOOTH's *Paedobaptist Examined*. Again, Slicer says, p. 329, " In every case which I have examined of the Paedobaptist authorities, quoted by Mr. Broaddus, I have found the remark of Peter Edwards (in regard to Booth) to hold good, that is, 'that those are *made to concede* what they *never meant to concede.*'"

Let me add another statement from Currie's "Catechism of Baptism," pp. 53 and 54. "Do immersionists quote other divines in support of the immersionist creed? Immersionist writers sometimes give extracts from others who are prominent affusionists" (that is, who are advocates of, and administer baptism by, sprinkling) "which appear to favour the immersionist idea; and these extracts, being disconnected from the context, have frequently misrepresented the views of their authors. Dr. Cramp selects from some divines a sentence or more that appears to favour his theory. He conceals what the writer says in immediate connection with the part quoted, and which explains or qualifies it, and thus misrepresents his author. He thus misrepresents John Wesley, Isaac Watts, Adam Clarke, George Whitefield, Thomas Chalmers, Martin Luther, and others." Let us now return to Booth's quotation of Deylingius.]

Now how could Cramp and Pengilly, in the face of that statement of Deylingius not to say more, which was there in Booth before their eyes, honestly make such affirmations about the Greek church never baptizing by affusion or sprinkling. They evidently wish their readers to believe that that church ever baptized by immersion only, which is not the fact, and hence they adduce no testimony at their hand to the contrary. That would defeat their object; that is, the truth would; so THE TRUTH is withheld, and something else, not true, is substituted. And there is *Huber.* Why not quote him as Currie does? Need I ask why? Their manner of treating Baxter, Clarke, Wesley, and now the Greek church, which I have exhibited to you, will sufficiently show their ruling motive.

6. But yet let us proceed to some more instances, and again we will return to the illustrious RICHARD BAXTER.

Pengilly's Scripture Guide to Baptism, p. 25, says: "Mr. Baxter has a very forcible passage on the same place, as follows, viz.: '*Go, disciple me all nations, baptizing them.* As for those who say they are discipled by baptizing, and not before baptizing, they speak not the sense of the text; nor that which is true or rational; else why should one be baptized more than another? 'This is not like some occasional historical mention of baptism; but it is the very commission of Christ to His apostles for preaching and baptizing; and purposely expresseth their several works in their several places and order. Their *first* task is by teaching to make disciples, which are, by Mark, called believers. The *second* work is to baptize them, whereto is annexed the promise of their salvation. The *third* work is to teach them all other things which are afterwards to be learned in the school of Christ. To contemn this order is to renounce all rules of order; for where can we expect to find it if not here? I profess my conscience is fully satisfied, from the text, that it is one sort of faith, *even saving*, that MUST GO BEFORE BAPTISM; and the profession whereof the minister must expect.'—*In Paedobaptist Examined*, vol. ii, p. 270." Note here that this is a professed quotation from Baxter, taken by Pengilly, not from Baxter's works direct, but from Booth's *Paedobaptist Examined*, second-hand. At this rate (and it is a very prevalent rate), if Booth err, and be unjust, or untruthful, in any case, Pengilly and many others contentedly repeat the same as all right. But why should Pengilly, who sets himself to write a book for the Baptist Publication Society, to be circulated cheaply many years among myriads, if possible—why should he not consult Baxter, &c., for himself, without taking the quotation from another. Baxter is easily accessible to such writers.

The object of Pengilly in this quotation is to establish that infants, as unbelievers, ought not to be baptized; and he cites Baxter, as quoted, to show that *he* also was of the same mind. Again, on page 44, he introduces him for the same object, namely, as against infant baptism, thus: "Mr. Baxter. ('The appeal he makes to Mr. Blake in this place,' remarks Pengilly here, 'might be made with all confidence to every Paedobaptist.') "I conclude (Baxter says) that all examples of baptism in Scripture do mention only the administration of it to the professors of saving faith; and the precepts give us no other direction. And I provoke Mr. Blake, as far as is seemly for me to do, to name ONE PRECEPT OR EXAMPLE for baptizing any other, and make it good if he can." *Disput. of Right to Sacram.*, p. 156. *In Paedobaptist Examined*, vol. ii. p. 29." This is also from Booth.

Now, to begin with, is it not strange to find Baxter, a genuine leading Presbyterian and infant Baptist, represented as quite opposed to the baptism of infants? What kind of a man in moral principle could he be? Honest, godly? A Baptist who quotes the like will say, as the Baptist minister here does, 'You may think this strange inconsistency in them, and so do I, but I have to state the facts. I cannot help their inconsistency.' Yes, the celebrated author of "The Saints' Rest," &c., &c., with many other godly men, are represented as strenuously denouncing others for teaching and doing what they habitually advocated and administered themselves without pause! But supposing these two quotations quite correct so far as they are given, may it not be that Baxter is speaking of adult baptism, apart from the subject of infants altogether, and is opposing those who advocated indiscriminate baptism of adults as the first means of making disciples; for in England, &c., there were and are such advocates. But Pengilly or Booth does not breathe a word of the connection in which the words occur. Baptists, like others, often say, that faith in Christ is necessary to salvation without specifying that they mean adults. Would they think it or would it be fair, to quote this from them to prove that they hold that no infants—since they are incapable of faith—can be saved? For they generally teach that all infants dying in infancy are saved—that is, without faith. They would reply, they were not speaking of infants, but meant those by age capable of faith; which would be a right reply. But they don't do that justice to others in the matter of baptism.

Let me now quote you Baxter's doctrine on the point in question from another source here in my hand, namely, "The Select Works of Rev. Matthew Henry" (the great commentator), whom I am sure, brethren, you will regard as a reliable authority for fair quotation. He was also a cotemporary of Baxter. In his "Treatise on Baptism" here, chap. iii, ques. 2, he says, "The Church of England concludes, concerning every baptized child, that it is regenerated and born again. In opposition to which Mr. BAXTER pleads (the following are Baxter's own words), "That baptism was not instituted to be a seal of the absolute promise of the first special grace, '*I will give them a new heart*,' but to be a seal of the covenant, properly so called, wherein God engageth himself, conditionally, to be our God; and therefore it (baptism) seals, TO THE INFANTS OF BELIEVERS, the promise of salvation, so as to be a means of conferring the benefit of salvation upon them, not as a physical, or hyperphysical instrument, but only as a moral instrument; by sealing and so conveying a legal right, which is AFTERWARDS improvable, as a means of working a real change upon the souls of those who have faith and the use of reason."

Observe here. *Baxter* says, "Baptism seals to the *infants* of believers," &c., &c., "which is *afterwards improvable* as a means," &c. Surely, then, he was not an advocate against infant baptism; and yet Pengilly, in those two quotations of his, so represents him out of Booth's work. We have therefore between him and Cramp a remarkable spectacle! Cramp, as I have shown you, in his "Baptist History," (page 275), quotes Baxter to show how strong he was against immersion, in which he affirms IMMERSION to be "no ordinance of God, but a most heinous sin." Then, in his other book, his "Catechism" (page 48), when he has an opposite object—to strengthen his argument in favour of immersion by the influence of great Paedobaptist names—he quotes Baxter (without stating anything of the place he quotes from) as saying, "In *our* baptism *we are dipped* under the water," and never breathes a word to the readers of that book that he had written *very* strongly against dipping. Then Pengilly and Booth complete the position by making out, from his lips, that he was opposed also to the baptism of infants, and wrote strongly against it. And yet the facts remain matter of history—of which his many excellent volumes, still accessible, are abundant evidence—that he was a Presbyterian, and, like other Presbyterians, was NOT "dipped under the water," nor re-baptized; administered the ordinance by sprinkling, not immersion; did so to infants, and *advocated* it as an ordinance of God, and no sin, but a duty and a privilege; was an eminently godly minister of Christ, and died as he lived, a Presbyterian Paedobaptist Christian. Do not the Baptists greatly mislead their readers and hearers? What kind of tree is it that produces such fruit? Is it of God? Can he approve? To what kind of religion does it lead?

7. MATTHEW HENRY is the next great Paedobaptist name enlisted by the Baptist leaders in their cause that I will consider,—the same I have been reading from to you in vindication of his cotemporary, the great Baxter. The greater the men the better, and Henry's is indeed a name of renown.

Pengilly, in his "Scripture Guide to Baptism" (page 28), cites Acts ii, 38, 39, where Peter, on the day of Pentecost, said to those who were pricked in their hearts, "Repent and be baptized, every one of you, in the name of Jesus Christ, for the remission of sins, and ye shall receive the gift of the Holy Ghost: For the promise is to you and to your children, and to all that are afar off, *even as many as the Lord our God shall call.*" In commenting on this for the Baptists' object, Pengilly says, "The promise to which the apostle alludes (in verse 39) has *no relation to infant* children." He gives some reasons for this assertion, and then cites, next page, some professed quotations from Paedobaptist writers, as being of the same mind with him in that assertion. In this way he adduces M. Henry thus: "MATTHEW HENRY (who is then quoted as saying), 'To this general the following limitations must refer, *even as many of them*, as many particular persons in each nation, *as the Lord our God shall call* effectually into the fellowship of Jesus Christ.'—*Exposition* of the place." This is the whole quoted from Henry on the verses in question. If Henry says anything more bearing on baptism of infants, which is the subject in question, or says anything in that way, on verse 38—"For the promise is to you and to your children," it does not appear in Pengilly. He professes to give Henry's real mind on the matter as to what these passages refer, as agreeing with his own. That is, of course, his profession to his readers, and those who trust him will accept his testimony as reliable; and does he not even name the place in Henry's Commentary where the quotation is from? Does not that look like a man who is fair? It is true, the FEW who have Henry's Commentary can look it up and see, only even they may think it needless; trusting that, no doubt, the quotation is all right; whilst the great majority who have it not will have to trust Pengilly in this, as in other cases. Alas, how he betrays them! Let us see. I have Henry's Commentary here before me on the place referred to; the words quoted are literally correct, *so far as they go*, yet, as I will show, still he is GROSSLY misquoted, misrepresented. Here we have a specimen of making a Paedobaptist writer appear, from his own lips, to support a doctrine he even, IN THE VERY PLACE, specifically *disowns*, and condemns one he *distinctly* and *repeatedly* ADVOCATES.

[Let me also remind you that Mr. Carnes, the Baptist minister, this same evening, after I had read you from Henry what I will now again place before you, stated on this in his reply, that what I read you from him only made Pengilly's statement and position stronger! He also repeated the same thing the following Wednesday, in the Baptist church, and would not allow me a reply at my request. Well, keep in mind this statement now, as Henry is set before you by me.]

Pengilly affirms that the promise alluded to in those verses "has *no* relation to *infant* children," and quotes Henry, on the place, in proof, as I have given you. Listen now to this from Henry in that SAME place, and see if Pengilly's assertion is made stronger by it: (Acts ii. 38, 39), "All that receive the remission of sins, receive the gift of the Holy Ghost; all that are justified and sanctified. *Your children shall* STILL *have, as they have had*, an interest in the covenant, and A TITLE TO the EXTERNAL SEAL of it. Come over to Christ to receive those inestimable benefits; for the promise of the remission of sins and the gift of the Holy Ghost is *to you and to your children*. It was very express (Isa. xliv. 3), 'I will pour my spirit upon thy seed;' and (Isa. lix. 21), 'My spirit and my word shall not depart from thy seed, and thy seed's seed.' When God took Abraham into covenant, He said, 'I will be a God to thee, and to thy seed' (Genesis xvii. 7); and, accordingly, every Israelite had his son circumcised at eight days old. Now it is proper for an Israelite, when he is by baptism to come into a new dispensation of this covenant, to ask, 'What must be done with my children? Must they be thrown out, or taken in with me?' 'Taken in,' says Peter, 'by all means; for the promise, that great promise of God's being to you a God, is as much to you *and to your children* now as ever it was. Though the promise is still extended to your children as it has been, yet it is not, as it has been, confined to you and them; but the benefit of it is *designed* for *all that are afar off;*' we may add, AND THEIR CHILDREN, for the blessing of Abraham comes upon the Gentiles through Jesus Christ (Gal. iii. 14). The promise had long pertained to the Israelites (Rom. ix. 4), but now it is sent to *those that are afar off*, the remotest nations of the Gentiles, and every one of them, too, 'all that are afar off.' (Here follow now the words quoted by Pengilly.) To this general the following limitation must refer: *Even as many of them*, as many particular persons in each nation, *as the Lord our God shall call* effectually into the fellowship of Jesus Christ."

In having what Henry did say correctly before you, brethren, you can see Pengilly's (and other Baptist writers') mode of manipulation. To make the reader believe (what you now see is very untrue) that the great Henry agrees with him (and all Baptists) that the promise spoken of in those verses " has no relation to infant children," nor to their being " deemed proper subjects of infant baptism," he quotes Henry *on another connected point*, and *leaves out* all that he does say on *the point in question*, without breathing a whisper that Henry does so at all. And how many Baptists and others that read Pengilly, or hear him quoted from by Baptist ministers in their proselytising efforts, as we heard Mr. Carnes do last Sabbath at much length—how many such will be told or come to know the genuine truth about Henry, &c., &c. Other Baptists are just as silent on it; and no doubt very many believe such misrepresentations without suspicion or desire or ability (not having the means within reach) to investigate.

[And what now will you think of the Baptist minister, Mr. Carnes's repeated affirmations that those additional quotations from Henry only strengthened Pengilly's representation of Henry's views. You may perceive a reason in these assertions for his persistent refusal to allow me the liberty of reply. HE KNEW I had several such sayings of his that I could clear up at once, which he could not stand before.]

8. MATTHEW HENRY once more AND OTHERS in a group.

Pengilly (same book as before) says, page 54: " If the New Testament does not afford an authority for infant baptism, upon what grounds do Paedobaptist divines practice and defend it? * * Many learned writers, as well as churches, have expressed their views upon this inquiry. Mr. Wall, Mr. Hammond, and many others, hold that the practice of 'Judish proselyte baptism' is the *foundation* of the Christian rite, and as infants received the former, so they should the latter; but Mr. Owen, Mr. Jennings, and others, have *proved* that no such practice existed among the Jews to afford such a pattern till generations after Christ. Sir N. Knatchbull assumes *circumcision* as the proper foundation. 'Beza, and, after him, Mr. Doddridge and others, considered the *holiness* of the children of believers as making them proper subjects. Mr. Matthew Henry and Mr. Dwight contended that '*the profession of faith made by the parents,*' to be their children's right. Mr. H. F. Burder affirms, 'The identical principle which pervades and unites the whole of the argument is, that infants are to be baptised *solely* on the ground of *connection with their parents,*'" &c. In a note at bottom, Pengilly refers for proof to Henry's Treatise on Baptism, Dwight's Theology, &c. Now, what is to be noted here is, that Pengilly represents those eminent Paedobaptists as differing from each other on these various grounds. That while Knatchbull, for example, assumes circumcision, he differs in this from Doddridge, who, on his part, says: No, circumcision is not the ground of infant baptism; it is the *holiness* of the children of believers. While, again, Henry and Dwight differ from both the preceding, and, refusing to acknowledge circumcision or holiness, say it is "the profession of faith made by their parents." And so on of all. This is what he wishes to impress upon his readers, and he introduces his quotations here with the statement, "Their grounds are various and contradictory."

Now, of these writers I have only Doddridge, Henry and Dwight at hand, and I find EACH of them *completely misrepresented*. Doddridge, in the 5th vol. of his works before me (lectures cciii., cciv., ccv.), instead of confining himself to "*the holiness*" as *the* ground for infant baptism (in the sense of federal holiness as in 1 Cor. vii. 14), not only gives that, but *also* circumcision, the connection of children with their believing parents, and the profession of faith made by their parents, &c., &c., *all* as arguments and reasons for it in Scripture. Henry, in his "Treatise on Baptism," now before me, chap. ii., proves the title of infants to baptism, not merely or only from the profession of faith made by their parents, *but also* from their federal holiness, from the Abrahamic covenant and circumcision, and several other reasons. In like manner, Dwight, in his Theology (which is before me), sermons clvii. clviii., *does the same thing*, proving *all those* various grounds, and others also, at length. And had I the other writers referred to—Wall, Hammond, &c., I have no doubt at all but they would be found in harmony with these. And yet Pengilly picks one argument for infant baptism from one writer, another argument from a second, another from a third, and so on, and says to his readers, See how these infant Baptists DIFFER from each other on the subject; there are different arguments; how hard it is to prove infant baptism when they have such opposing views. While after all, the fact is, each of them holds the argument attributed to him and *those attributed to the others* AS WELL; there being *several* reasons or proofs of the same thing, which they all use in common.

Besides the quotations, &c., which I have now proven to be gross misrepresentations of the "pious fraud" and Jesuitical class, there are still quite a number in Pengilly, Cramp, and other Baptist books in common circulation, which I can prove similarly. Of a considerable number, again, I have not the Paedobaptist books referred to (which will be the case still more with most readers and hearers), by which, if I had, I could see a similar abuse of them, it may be most reasonably presumed. I will now close the list on this division of my Lecture by another somewhat different in kind, viz.:—

Pengilly's argument to prove that John's baptism was by immersion, in (page 14 of) his "Scripture Guide to Baptism."

He says: "We should notice the *place* where John administered this ordinance. It was 'the river Jordan.' If, in reference to the people of Jerusalem, a situation where water might easily be obtained for sprinkling or pouring, was what John required, we read of our Lord at this place directing the man that was born blind to go and 'wash in the pool of Siloam;' so we read of the 'pool called Bethesda,' and 'the brook Cedron,' all *in* or *near* Jerusalem (and we read of others in the Old Testament); and without doubt at some of them the penitent Jews of that city and neighborhood might have received the ordinance, *if such* were the mode by which John administered it; and it CANNOT REASONABLY BE IMAGINED he would have REQUIRED those persons to go the distance of several miles *for the convenience* of the river Jordan; *more reasonable* to suppose he would have baptized in every town and village where his ministry had its intended effect; and, ESPECIALLY, at or near the METROPOLIS. This strongly favours the opinion that IMMERSION was the mode. Thus: (and here follows, in his usual plan, a number of professed quotations from Paedobaptists to confirm this reasoning from their writings.)

In short, the argument here is, that if "especially at or near the metropolis," Jerusalem, John had had conveniences for baptizing his penitents by *immersion*, it *cannot* be *reasonably* imagined he would *not* have done so there. But instead of that, and because he could *not* obtain that convenience *there*, he THEREFORE *required* those persons to go the distance of several miles to Jordan, that he might thus be able to immerse them. Observe the force of the argument is, he obliged them to go to the Jordan, BECAUSE he *could not find a suitable place* AT or NEAR JERUSALEM for IMMERSION, while it is admitted, or contended, that he could have had at or near Jerusalem conveniences sufficient for sprinkling or pouring.

I may remark preliminarily that John might have had (and we have no doubt had) other reasons, apart from the water required for baptism, for preaching and abiding "in the wilderness," rather than in Jerusalem and other towns, as Jesus had wise reasons for spending his time chiefly in Galilee rather than in Judea and Jerusalem. But, apart from this, let us allow to Pengilly, meanwhile, the full force of his reasoning, and suppose John's only reason for going to the Jordan was for the means of immersion. His Baptist readers will likely accept his argument as conclusive, meanwhile, and it will be hoped that Paedobaptist readers and hearers will accept it also as just and convincing. Be it so. The argument is proposed, of course, as sound in the facts and reasoning, Pengilly being the witness. That being granted, can Baptists or others object if I transfer it as it is, without disturbance or alteration, from John's baptism to the baptisms in the same Jerusalem, on the day of Pentecost, when (Acts ii : 41) 8,000 were baptized by the apostles ? Then how will it operate? If John could not find conveniences for immersion in or near Jerusalem, neither could *they*; and they had a great multitude to baptize in that one day. If John went to Jordan, as is here said, because nearer than that to Jerusalem there was no place suitable for his alleged purpose, then it follows that, since the apostles baptized the 8,000 in Jerusalem—"at or near it"—therefore they did not baptize by immersion, but by sprinkling, or pouring. Now that is just one of our arguments as to their inability to immerse the 3,000 there. It is known there was not convenience for that. But will the Baptists be willing to admit, now, Pengilly's assertions and reasoning on the insufficiency of water in Jerusalem, when we maintain the *same thing* of the day of Pentecost, there, as one of our proofs that the 8,000 could not have been immersed? O, NO. In this connection they feel bound to see plenty of water for immersion at or near Jerusalem, as the 8,000 were baptized there, and all the while the Baptist Publication Society still publishes and circulates in its books, as in Pengilly's, that *John* brought the people to the Jordan, "because at or near Jerusalem especially," while there was water enough available for sprinkling, there was not sufficient for immersion there.

But in addition to the question of the insufficiency of water, there were other obstacles enough to prevent the immersion of the 3,000. One of them was this : The places of water were all of them in the possesssion of the numerous and bitter enemies of Christ (whom they had very recently crucified) and of his disciples and their doctrine and baptism. The feast of Pentecost was one of the three annual feasts on which the Lord had required in the law all the males of the Jewish race to appear before him at his house in Jerusalem (Exod. xxii. 14–17 ; Deut. xvi. 16). Consequently, on this occasion, there were present in that city not only the usual large population of hundreds of thousands, with their priests, scribes, pharisees and rulers, but a vast number besides from Judea, Galilee, and "every nation under heaven," (Acts ii. 5–11), all animated on such an occasion with anti-christian religious fervour and zeal. Now, would they—filled, too, as they were with animosity against the disciples of the Messiah—would they allow the water they needed for food, and drink, and religious purposes, to be polluted in the ordinary and (as they would deem) in the religious sense, by the immersion in it, at one time, too, of thirty hundred of the hated sect of the Nazarenes? But there is no mention in the Acts, or elsewhere, of the shadow of a commotion or objection from the Jews on that subject, the absence of which is itself a proof of our position that there was no immersion on the occasion. Other reasons might be added. Let this suffice.

I now bring this part of my subject to a close. I have given you evidence to show that Baptist writers, under the auspices of the Baptist Publication Societies, etc., deal freely and systematically in misquotations and misrepresentations of the views of infant-Baptist writers; which also Baptist ministers and people most diligently repeat and circulate. It is for you to judge, brethren, whether I have done so sufficiently. And these given you are only a few specimens. I do not wonder that those who are brought up from youth under such influences, and others related to other communions, but who are not acquainted with the true merits of the question, should be led to regard the Anabaptist doctrines as right, when they read and hear their special pleading, without, at the same time, the opportunity of hearing the other side from those who know and fairly exhibit it. It is not too much to say that the great body of that denomination of Christians,—ministers and people—form their views and belief from a few leading books, such as Pengilly and Cramp, or, what is the same, from the statements of such books repeated orally by those who take all as genuine fact, without inquiring for themselves into the original works referred to, and other independent sources of information. Many—as the common people—cannot do so from the want of the necessary learning, and the many different books, the time, and expense. But where misrepresentation is used as a means of securing the object in view, such trouble, expense, and ability are necessary to find it out, and those who don't do this, or learn the facts from those who do, are very liable to be deceived, and in this matter are deceived. Such a result will follow in any connection. Let an able lawyer, or several such, on one side of a cause, exert their abilities as special pleaders, to bring forward, withhold, and manage the evidence as they please before a jury, and the evidence on the other side not be heard or known, except as given by those who strain every nerve to get judgment against it; would not justice usually miscarry if that were the way, and the jury or audience be often led to believe the worse to be the better cause? Nor would truth and right be safe even in the hands of men, on the whole, honestly inclined, For they also are liable to be misled and mistaken. Such is human frailty, even in good men, and in proportion as the bias is strong in favour of one side of things, there is a proportionate tendency to receive, believe, and use, without being as particular as truth requires, statements on the authority of others, and arguments that appear fitted in their nature to serve the object in view. Looking at the way the Baptist people and common ministers get their great question set before them, by special pleading leaders, and remembering the influence of bias in the too ready acceptance by frail humanity of what we favour, I don't wonder at their belief, nor at their common and great zeal, so much out of proportion to the real value of the question,—they are so constantly impressed and stirred up on it to such extent, by those who are over them, and by each other, to do all they can to get their opinions propagated, that considering frail and erroneously inclined, plastic human nature, and the amount of real ignorance, and power of the ambition of success, and other mutual excitements, few are able to resist the constant pressure of such influences, but are carried by their convictions and feelings along an impetuous current. To some onlookers and themselves, such zeal may appear an evidence of rectitude of belief, and certainly it is proof of their attaching immense importance to their theory of the baptism of water. But need I say that zeal may be great and wide-spread and yet 'not according to knowledge' of truth or true religion. Even Rome can succeed in bringing over to her creed those who don't know better. And those brought up under her management from youth, as also and especially, those she may have brought over, are very zealous even to fanaticism in her cause as being that of truth and God. .

My last remark before leaving this subject is : Baptists are in the habit of saying they make their appeals to the Word of God alone, and not to the views and doctrines of the fathers, or uninspired men. Yet, while this is constantly repeated, I find in their books on Baptism they very much forget and abuse this wholesome rule ; for they have very great fondness for quotations from uninspired men to support their ideas. Now, in this, what is the difference between the ancient and modern fathers ? If the one class is not to be appealed to, why the others ? Suppose that out of the thousands of infant-baptist writers of eminent name, who are opposed completely to Anabaptism as unscriptural, a number of infant-baptists, . so-called, were to be found agreeing with the Baptists against the baptism of infants as unscriptural, and they, mark, infant baptizers, at the same time, all the while till their death, or against sprinkling as unscriptural, and they all the while baptizing still by sprinkling, would their statements of that nature deserve to be regarded of special value in deciding the truth of the Scripture in the case ? But I have shown you that even in making professed quotations from such, the Baptist denomination is not so scrupulous and truthful as she ought to be, but certainly violates greatly the ninth Commandment in bearing false witness against her Paedobaptist brethren, by misrepresenting them; which is repeated, to her great guilt, over and over again, in her name and by her authority, by thousands of lips, and year after year continually.

[In the foregoing narration of lecture, the various topics and incidents are given as in the meeting, with this difference here, that the reasoning on several is stated more fully, and some of the counter-quotations from Paedobaptist works are more extended, no new matter being introduced. The oral delivery being in fewer words, did not take so long as the foregoing would. At this stage of the lecture the lecturer paused, and said that although Mr. Carnes—the Baptist minister present—had stated at the beginning of the meeting, in reply to his inquiry, as was understood, that he meant not to reply to this lecture to-night, yet, he may have changed his mind since; and if so, he would give him opportunity now if he wished it. But if he did not wish this, and if the meeting were not too tired, but would like him to go on to the next division of his lecture—the Early Church History of Infant Baptism—he would do so. Upon this many voices cried, "Go on! Go on!" and so did Mr. Carnes; the lecturer thereupon entered on the next division.]

Part II.

THE EARLY CHURCH HISTORY OF INFANT BAPTISM.

As before stated it has been constantly asserted that Infant Baptism is a relic of the Church of Rome. Into this we will now inquire. In doing so we will, of course, have to trace the history of the question as near to the apostolic age of the first century as we can find authentic evidence. It is admitted on all sides that the Apostle John died about A.D. 100, or at the very close of the first century. It is to be remembered that in those early periods there were no books printed by types as now,—all was done with the pen, which was a very laborious and expensive process, and greatly limited the number and circulation of the writings. Also, education among the people was very limited in extent and degree. And for some time after the apostles' day the occasions for writing books and the number of writers were not so many as in subsequent centuries, when the Church's borders became more enlarged, the number able and willing to serve as instructors proportionately increased, the restraints of hostile civil powers removed, and when contentions for the faith against heresies had become numerous and widespread. In the second and third centuries, the powers of civil government being in the hands of the heathen, Christians were subject to many persecutions, and their writings, not nearly so numerous as in after centuries, were many of them lost. In fact not many such writings remain to us. And only a few of these touch on baptism.

In our present investigation the Baptist books I will use of Dr. Cramp's, you will understand to be the same "Baptist History" and "Catechism on Baptism" of his I have been using before; and that of Pengilly—will be his "Scripture Guide to Baptism." I mention this now to save time by not having to repeat their titles in full when I refer to them, but simply Cramp's Baptist History, or History, and his Catechism, and simply, Pengilly.

The Baptist bias from their side of the question at issue, is to darken and explain away the evidence that may be adduced in favour of our views; also to suppress and misrepresent the facts in evidence. This temptation, I have to say is freely yielded to in proportion to the difficulties they meet with in maintaining the Baptist position. We will see how it leads them to adopt a similar policy to that we have already seen, in the first part of the lecture. A cause whose advocacy feels pressed to resort, and that systematically from beginning to end, to such policy is not of God and His Word. If the Baptist cause did not require this method of defence and propagation, they would not, of course, resort to it.

As the early Christian writers did not write in English, you understand, but in the Latin and Greek languages, etc., the right translation of words bearing on the matters of controversy, is often a question of dispute. Hence, in our inquiry, if I use the translations the Baptist themselves acknowledge and give as correct, there will be no room for objection to them from their side. This plan I will follow.

Of the earliest historical evidence after the apostles, on this subject, Cramp says in his History, p. 10 :—" The 'Apostolic Fathers' first claim attention. They are: Barnabas, Hermas, Clement of Rome, Ignatius, and Polycarp. They contain *no* reference to the subject now before us." These are called 'Apostolic Fathers,' I may explain, because they, at least the first four, lived in the apostles' time, the first two having been fellow-labourers of Paul's (Acts xiii; Rom. xvi. 14).

The next Christian writer is JUSTIN MARTYR. Pengilly says (p. 74), he wrote the "Apology for Christians, addressed to the Emperor, the Senate, and people of Rome" (from which I am about to give you extracts), "about A.D. 140," that is, only about forty years after the apostle John. Of him says Cramp in his History, p. 12, "Justin

Martyr was a philosophic Christian. He was put to death at Rome A.D. 166" (or twenty-six years after his 'Apology'). "In his first 'Apology,' addressed to the Emperor Marcus Aurelius, he gives the following account of baptism as practised in his days:—' As many as are persuaded and believe that what we teach is true, and undertake to conform their lives to our doctrine, are instructed to fast and pray, and entreat from God the remission of their past sins, we fasting and praying together with them. They are then conducted by us to a place where there is water, and are regenerated in the same manner in which we ourselves were regenerated. FOR THEY ARE THEN WASHED *in the name of* God the Father, and Lord of the Universe, and of our Saviour Jesus Christ, and of the Holy Spirit.'" Justin wrote in Greek, and the above, Cramp gives as a correct translation. Pengilly, in p. 74, gives a translation of the same passage, *with a sentence more* at the *beginning*, which is (Justin being the speaker), —" I will now declare to you also after what manner WE, being made anew by Christ, HAVE DEDICATED OURSELVES to God," etc. The subject of *this* passage, it thus appears, is SELF-dedication to God by baptism, in those days of constant and numerous conversions of adult heathens to Christ. And is a DIFFERENT subject from that of the dedication by Christian parents of *their offspring*. Justin had been himself a heathen.

In Pengilly, further, there is a noteworthy difference of words from Cramp's in the last two sentences, to which I wish particular attention. Cramp's is, "They are then conducted by us to a place where there is water, and are REGENERATED in the SAME MANNER in which WE WERE OURSELVES REGENERATED. For they are then washed in the name of God the Father," etc. In Pengilly it is, "Then we bring them to some place where there is water, and they are BAPTIZED by the SAME WAY OF BAPTISM by which we were BAPTIZED; for they are washed (*en to udati*) *in the water* in the name of God the Father," etc. Here the words "(*en to udati*) in the water," are not in Cramp's, nor in it in his "Catechism," p. 16. But what I wish attended to in particular is, that where the one gives the rendering "regenerated" the other, in each case instead, uses the word "baptized." And in the extract from Cramp it is plain that Justin affirms regeneration to have been effected by baptism, by being "washed in the name of the" Trinity. In Murdock and Seaton Reid's Mosheim's Ecclesiastical History, (edition 1852, p. 75, note) for example, will be found a translation of a larger portion of this passage, where also the two terms, "regenerated" and "baptized" are given as used synonymously, referring to the same act. And Cramp and Pengilly, two leading Baptist authorities, taken together, agree therewith. On this I will read a sentence from Schaff's History of the Christian Church, vol. I, p. 395. "The IDEA of Baptism. This ordinance was regarded in the ancient church as the sacrament of conversion and regeneration. Tertullian (of A.D. 200) describes its effects thus:—'The soul becomes transformed through regeneration by water and power from above,'" etc. On this point, however, both sides are agreed. And Cramp's quotation from Justin Martyr, of itself, makes that plain. With these observations I leave this point at present.

After giving the quotation from Justin, Cramp then adds, "Observe the manner in which he speaks of baptism. The candidates are those who are 'persuaded' and 'believe;' and the ordinance is administered, not by sprinkling, but by the water of immersion." Now, I ask you, brethren, to observe that Justin does not speak, as Cramp alleges, of immersion. There is no such word in the passage. It is "They are then *washed* in the name of God the Father," etc. Cramp is at no difficulty in proving his point. He leaves it as so proved, with those words. The word "washed" with him necessarily means immersion. The *mode* of baptism is not my subject to-night, but I will pause a moment on it here. On the same principle, were some Baptist, or Cramp himself, to read in our Presbyterian Shorter Catechism, "Baptism is a sacrament, wherein the *washing* with water in the name of the Father, and of the Son, and of the Holy Ghost doth signify," etc., he would say, Here is sufficient proof that the Presbyterian Church of Britain, Canada, etc., etc., baptize by IMMERSION! These words, you observe, too, happen to be the same as Justin's. In Justin the sign, "baptism," is called by the name of the thing signified "regeneration," after the manner of the Apostles, and of the

Scriptures in general (Titus iii. 5; Rom. vi. 3–6; Acts xxii. 16; Math. xxvi. 26, etc.). It is to be understood, of course, that the *washing* of baptism is not a literal washing to remove the "filth of the flesh," but symbolical. In Rev. i. 5, believers are said to be 'washed from their sins in the blood of Christ,' and Paul calls the symbolical sign of that "the blood of sprinkling," (Heb. xii. 24). David, in Psalm li., says, "Purge me with hyssop and I shall be clean; yea, *wash* Thou me," etc. Does he mean immersion there as the symbolical act? We know the hyssop was used for sprinkling. Pengilly has "*(en to udati) in the water.*" The italics are his own. He wishes by these Greek words, and his rendering of them, to make out the idea of immersion. Even "*in* the water," added to what precedes, does not *prove* that. But *he translates* the Greek *en*, as if it *unquestionably* means "in," and nothing else. In Mosheim, p. 75, note, before mentioned, it is rendered by "with," in this same passage. But hear the leading Baptist writer, Dr. Carson, "I do not deny that *en* may be translated *with*." (On Baptism, p. 121.) In the recent *Baptist* translation of the New Testament now before me, it is often rendered "with," because they could not make sense by *in*, in the places, as Matt. vii. 6., "nor cast your pearls before the swine, lest they trample them *with* (*en*) their feet." So also, ch. vii. 1; xx. 15; xxv. 16; xxvi. 52, "all they that take the sword shall perish with (*en*) the sword," and a host of others.

But Justin says, "They are conducted by us to a place where there is water." Well, so far as those words go, immersion is not indicated. When I baptize children in our church they are brought to a place where there is water, viz.: to the baptismal font, as it is called, from which I sprinkle water upon them. In the description I read you from Huber (page 19) of the four Greek church baptisms he witnessed, he tells that "a table stood in the middle (of the room) with a BASIN on it. The priest was then sent for, who, upon entering the room, was received by the father of the infant and LED TO THE BAPTISMAL WATER, which he consecrated by a short prayer," etc. The child was afterwards sprinkled by dropping some water out of the basin on its forehead. As well, then, to make out immersion from the words (in capitals here) from Huber, as to say Justin's expression, "led by us to a place where there is water," is proof of immersion. Small evidence goes far on their own side, but you will see soon, and much, a different disposition with really strong evidence on what they are opposed to.

As to those Justin here speaks of as first "believing" and being "persuaded" of the truth of what they are taught, observe, he is describing to the heathen emperor, senate, and people, outside of the Christian church how converts dedicated THEMSELVES to God. (Justin himself, and Christians in general, of that period, were at first avowed heathens or Jews). The sentence of Justin indicating that he was describing their "self-dedication" Cramp has left out; Pengilly has it in. In addressing heathens it was natural he would refer to the way *such* were admitted into the Christian church. But we will see infants soon.

In his History Cramp next refers to IRENÆUS, (p. 13,) of whom he says as follows :—" Irenæus became Bishop of Lyons in France A.D. 177 (or about forty years after Justin Martyr's Apology)' and died A.D. 202. He mentions baptism several times, and *seemingly* connects it with regeneration as Justin had done before him, in the passage just cited." In regard to Justin we have seen that there is no "seemingly" about his language; for he expressly connects the two together—'regenerated by baptism.' Irenæus spoke similarly, "connecting baptism with regeneration as Justin had done before him," Cramp himself being witness. Next, (in p. 14,) Cramp says:—" Two passages used to be quoted by Paedobaptist writers as testimonies in favour of INFANT baptism." Observe the sleight of hand he practises here in the introduction of these passages :—" Two passages *used* to be quoted," etc., plainly making an insinuation equal to an assertion; that Paedobaptist writers dont quote these now,—have given them up,—which is very untrue. They are regarded still, as they have always been, as weighty passages, and so will they be by you, brethren, I think, when they are before you. He goes on to say, "One of these is from Justin Martyr. He writes thus :—' Many men and many women, sixty and seventy years old, who *from* CHILDREN have been DISCIPLES of Christ, preserve their continence.' The other is from Irenæus. These are his words:—'He came to save sinners by himself; all I say WHO ARE REGENERATED by him unto God—INFANTS and children, and boys, and young men, and old men.'" On these, Cramp remarks, "But baptism is not mentioned in either of these passages, and modern critics have confessed that they afford no support to the Paedobaptist view." Then as the usual resort he gives a quotation from a German writer to confirm his remarks. His expression—"And modern critics have confessed," &c., is also misleading. It insinuates to the common reader that such is the confession of most or all modern critics, which is very untrue. But we are not to decide these cases by quotations from others, of which it would be easy to give abundance in support of the Paedobaptist view. We are not going to give up our own private judgment to a German writer, or Cramp, or *any* other. We have the materials for judgment before ourselves, which being set before you, brethren, from Baptist authorities are therefore indisputable. We have seen, and Baptists admit that Justin and Irenæus were accustomed to speak of baptism AS THE MEANS OF REGENERATION and as the same thing. In the former passage of Justin, he says those brought to the water "are regenerated in the same manner in which we were ourselves regenerated. FOR they are then washed in the name of the Father," &c. Pengilly uses the word "baptized" in his translation as a proper rendering of that term rendered "regenerated" by Cramp. And Irenæus is admitted by Cramp to "connect baptism with regeneration the same as Justin did before him." These things being so, will it do to say there is NO evidence at all in that passage from Irenæus about baptism, because the *word* baptism does not occur? Cramp and Pengilly, etc., have no difficulty at all in seeing and saying that in the first passage from Justin the baptism was by IMMERSION, although the word immersion does not occur in it; and, besides, no other expression in it means that. But here they cannot see any evidence in favour of baptism, just as if there was none at all in the connection always made between it and regeneration. Well, we had better in that case judge for ourselves. Irenæus, among the others—the "children, boys, young men and old men"—he specifies there, says, that "INFANTS are REGENERATED unto God."

He and Justin before him, and his cotemporary Tertullian and the subsequent writers always taught that it was by baptism regeneration was effected. It may be *reasonably concluded*, therefore, that in Irenæus' day—less than eighty years from the apostolic age—the practice of the Church was to baptize infants. Moreover, since on the known fact that baptism was held as the means of regeneration and equivalent to it, Pengilly uses the word " baptized " as the proper rendering in the former passage of Justin, of the word Cramp renders " regenerated," why not on the same principle render "regenerated" by "baptized" in this passage of Irenæus. It would then read " infants, etc., etc., are baptized unto God "—with the idea involved in that that thus " infants are regenerated unto God," so that in effect the one statement is the precise equivalent of the other.

I may remark here that our subject is not affected in the slightest by any evidence that those early or later writers had *erroneous* views of the nature of baptism, as really regenerating the baptized. *The* point is, they held and taught that baptism and regeneration went together as cause and effect,—to baptize was to regenerate, and to be regenerated was to be baptized.

The other passage of Justin's is differently given in Cramp's History from his Catechism, (p. 18,) where it is :—
" There are persons among us, both males and females, sixty, seventy years old, who, from children *were discipled to* Christ, and have remained pure." But in his History (p. 14)—*" Many* men and *many* women, sixty and seventy years old, who, from children *have been disciples of* Christ, preserve their continence." Between these two forms of the same passage there are, in some respects, distinct differences in meaning ; and more correctness ought to be in passages, the exact meaning of which is the subject of investigation. We have of course a choice between the two. His History is the latest work, and I take the passage given there, as presenting it most correctly. In his Catechism Cramp reasons thus :—" Baptism is not mentioned here, the word employed ('discipled ') implies the act of a conscious, intelligent being, capable of being taught and of reducing principles to practice, in which sense Justin himself uses the words in other parts of his writings." The idea of *the passage* is, not that the many men and

women were *under the process* of being "discipled to Christ," from children, but that "they had been disciples *of* Christ" *since then;*—had become disciples in their childhood. And the question is, whether Justin regarded any unregenerated person, young or old, as becoming a disciple by being regenerated. Did he consider *all* regenerated or born again by the spirit of Christ, to become, by that fact, disciples of Christ, as distinguished from the rest of the unregenerated portion of mankind? There is every reason to believe he did, as regeneration is that by which the dispositions and position of true discipleship is secured. Then as he held that baptism both regenerates and formally admits the baptized to the name of disciples or of the sheep of Christ's pasture,—to have become in childhood a disciple of Christ implies that they were baptized then to begin with, as baptism was held to be *the* means of regeneration. Cramp says further in his Catechism, "The expression 'from children' must therefore be understood to be equivalent to the modern phrase 'in early life,'"— that is, according to his view of the term "discipled." I admit that those words are a correct rendering of the original Greek, *ek paidon*, and that the term for children there, like our own word children, is often used for an age above infancy, but it must be admitted equally that it applies also like our word children, to *infants* as well. Thus in the New Testament, Matt. ii. 16: "Then Herod, when he saw that he was mocked of the wise men, was exceeding wroth, and sent forth and slew all the *children* that were in Bethlehem, and in all the coasts thereof, *from two years old* AND UNDER." The Greek word for "children," here, is the same as in Justin. Also Baptists use the term PAEDO-baptist to indicate those who baptize *infants*, which is the *same* Greek word prefixed to "baptist." Justin's expression therefore does not exclude the age of *earliest* infancy. Note, moreover, that he in the passage under review evidently lays emphasis on those words—that those aged people were disciples *from* their *childhood*. Keep in mind too, that his cotemporary, Irenæus declares that among others of all ages, "*infants*" (infantes) were also regenerated unto God through Christ, and that they both, etc., taught strongly that regeneration was effected by baptism. These things being so it cannot be truly said that this passage and that from Irenæus, I explained before, "afford no support to the Paedobaptist view," but the very reverse can be said. And they were very near the apostolic age.

The next witness on the subject is TERTULLIAN. In connection with his evidence on our subject there is particular interest, as he writes on it positively and at length. Consequently his utterances have been, and are regarded by both sides of much importance as to the history of the question, and been attended to correspondingly.

In the way of preparing his readers for the value he wishes them to attach to the evidence on the practice of infant-baptism, or "child"-baptism, as he calls it, which here appears, and to lead them to suppose it one of the departures from truth that began in that age, Cramp, in his History, first describes the times and Tertullian. Of him he says (p. 17), "Tertullian, for example, a Christian writer who flourished at the close of the second and commencement of the third century, declares the following spiritual blessings to be consequent upon baptism :—Remission from sins, deliverance from death, regeneration, and participation in the Holy Spirit. He calls it 'the sacrament of washing,' 'the blessed sacrament of water,' 'the laver of regeneration.'" In the next pages Cramp refers to other signs of the times, as indicating the progress and spread of human additions in religious worship, some of the corruptions of doctrine and worship that afterwards prevailed. I may add, what is admitted by all sides, that Tertullian ultimately became a disciple and advocate of one *Montanus*, a remarkable heretic, who gave himself out to be the Paraclete or Comforter whom the Saviour promised to send to His disciples after His ascension (John xiv. 16-17 ; xvi. 7-14). Mosheim (Eccles. Hist. Century II., chap. v., sec. 23, 24) concludes his account of Tertullian thus :—"Of all Montanus's followers, the most learned and distinguished was Tertullian, a man of genius, but austere and gloomy by nature ; who defended the cause of his preceptor by many energetic and severe publications." Montanus's heresy, besides its blasphemy, was very austere in nature. Much is made by Baptists of the fact that Tertullian opposed the baptism of infants ; on account of which he seems to be forgiven his other great failings, and much admired. For example, in my copy of Pengilly's "Scripture Guide to Baptism," (paper covers), on the inside page of each cover are printed (and issued along with the book, by the Baptist Publication Society, Philadelphia) "Historical Conclusions on Infant Baptism, by J. Torrey Smith;" from which I quote :—" In the beginning of the third century we find such controversy (on infant-baptism). And one clear note of remonstrance has sounded through all the intervening ages to our day, namely, that of *stout-hearted old Tertullian* (A.D. 200)." That is to say, though *all* historians affirm alike of him, (and six volumes of his writings are still extant) that he was very unsound in the faith, ultimately a great and pronounced heretic, and a rude, though able and zealous man after his own ideas; and J. Torrey Smith must have known all that (but the vast majority of his readers, of course, would not), yet, because he in some sort (to be seen yet) opposed infant-baptism, he is represented as one of the greatest and best of his day. Probably the motive in this is, by giving him (by misrepresentation) such a character, to impress the unlearned reader with the idea that infant-baptism must be unscriptural, and an innovation then, or such a good and noble man would not have opposed it. We will see Pengilly, while entirely silent as to his demerits, drawing what he intends as a strong argument from his faithfulness to Scripture, and that contrary to the evidence before *him* in the place quoted, which he does *not* give his readers, and we will see others similarly.

I will now set before you, from different sources, what Tertullian wrote on the question. And I have to state preliminarily that Baptist writers cannot, and DO NOT, deny the accuracy of the facts to be stated, but adopt the policy I have shown you in the first part of this lecture of giving only a part, suppressing the connected parts, and then giving meanings to what they quote quite different from the original writer's, which would be seen were the words of the writer in the immediate connection not withheld. Tertullian wrote a treatise on Baptism somewhat at length. His statements in it are now the subject of consideration.

The first account I will give you is from an excellent and able treatise on "Infant Baptism Scriptural and Reasonable: and Baptism by Sprinkling or Affusion, the most Suitable and Edifying Mode: by Samuel Miller, D.D., Professor of Ecclesiastical History and Church Government in the Theological Seminary at Princeton. New Jersey Presbyterian Board of Publication: Philadelphia." The price of this work (paper or other covers) is small, and it is well worth procuring. I will have occasion to refer to it frequently and will call it just " Miller."

In this work of Miller, p. 22, he says:—"Tertullian, about two hundred years after the birth of Christ [100 after the last of the apostles,] is the first man of whom we read in Ecclesiastical History, as speaking a word against infant-baptism; and he, while he recognises the existence and prevalence of the practice, and *expressly* recommends that infants be baptized, if they are not likely to survive the period of infancy; yet advises that, where there is a prospect of their living, baptism be delayed until a late period in life. But what was the reason of this advice? The *moment we look at* THE REASON, we see that it avails nothing to the cause in support of which it is sometimes produced. Tertullian adopted the superstitious idea, that baptism was accompanied with the remission of all past sins; and that sins committed AFTER baptism were PECULIARLY DANGEROUS. He therefore, advised, that not merely infants, [what follows Baptist writers omit mentioning, as if there were no such statements,] but young *men* and young *women;* and even *young widows* and *widowers* should postpone their baptism until the period of youthful appetite and passion should have passed. In short, he advised that, in all cases in which death was not likely to intervene, baptism be postponed, until the subjects of it should be arrived at a period of life, when they would no longer be in danger of being led astray by youthful lusts. And thus, for more than a century after the age of Tertullian, we find some of the most conspicuous converts to the Christian faith, postponing baptism till the close of life. Constantine the Great, we are told, though a professing Christian for many years before, was not baptized till after the commencement of his last illness. The same fact is recorded of a number of other distinguished converts to Christianity, about and after that time. But, surely, advice and facts of this kind make nothing in favour of the system of our Baptist brethren. Indeed, taken altogether, their historical bearing is strongly in favour of our system."

In confirmation of the portion which Baptist writers omit to set before their readers, I will quote from one or two historians. They each give the above account as to infants, but, as I will give that from Baptist authorities, I will not repeat it just now. The first I give is from the "History of the Apostolic Church, by Philip Schaff, Professor in the Theological Seminary at Mercersburg. T. & T. Clark, publishers, Edinburgh, 1854; Vol. II." He says, p. 270, "Tertullian holds an early baptism to be dangerous, because, according to his Montanistic notions, a mortal sin committed after baptism excludes for ever from the communion of the Church, and probably incurs eternal damnation. On this ground he advises not only children, but *even adults* also, who are yet unmarried and under no vow of chastity, to put off baptism until they are secure against temptation to gross carnal indulgence." Here he adds, in a note, an extract from Tertullian, which I will give, and then translate, "Non minore causa," says Tertullian, "innupti quoque procrastinandi, in quibus tentatio praeparata est tam virginibus per maturitatem, quam viduis per vacationem, donec aut nubant aut continentiae corroborentur,"—That is, "Nor is it from less (weighty) reason that those not in the marriage relation should also defer (baptism), in whom temptation is ready at hand as much to virgins through their maturity as to widows by their isolation, till they marry or are strongly confirmed in continence."

Next, "Hagenbach's History of Doctrines," (T. & T. Clark, Edinburgh, 1846), vol. I., p. 194. "From the opposition which Tertullian raised to infant-baptism (*de baptismo*, 18), it may be inferred that it was a customary practice in his times. He alleges the following reasons against it:—[I pass over these (as they will appear again) except this last, namely] 5. The great responsibility which the subject of baptism takes upon him. From the last mentioned reason he recommends to even grown-up persons, single persons, widows, etc., to delay baptism till they are either married or formed the firm resolution to live a single life."

Lastly on this. Three years ago I read over Tertullian's

Treatise on Baptism myself, both in the original Latin and in the English translation of the Fathers by Clark, Edinburgh, and can bear personal testimony to the complete accuracy to the account of it I have quoted from Miller, Schaff, and Hagenbach. The bearing of these points will appear again.

Let us now return to the Baptist writer, Cramp. In his History, p. 19, he says:—" The extension of the administration of baptism, in an unwarrantable manner, is referred to by Tertullian in his tract, '*De Baptismo*,' in terms of strong disapproval. Some persons had introduced children (NOT *infants*) to baptism, or advocated the administration of the ordinance to them. Tertullian indignantly reproves the practice. ' Let them come,' he says, ' when they are taught to whom they may come ; let them become Christians when they are able to know Christ. Why should this innocent age hasten to the remission of sins ?' " He continues : " Now, *is it not* OBVIOUS that Tertullian was entirely unacquainted with *infant* baptism, and that this children's baptism which then began first to be talked of, was regarded by him as an unauthorized innovation ? . . . The case is QUITE CLEAR, children, (NOT *infants*, but probably children *from* SIX to TEN *years* old) are first mentioned in connection with the ordinance at the beginning of the third century, and then with disapproval."

Note here : the forementioned *three* sentences of Tertullian's are all Cramp quotes from his treatise ; and immediately asks, " Now, is it not obvious," etc., and adds again :—" The case is quite clear." The " obvious " aim of all this will appear presently. Note further, how he has affirmed and repeated over and again that Tertullian did not refer to *infants* in what he wrote, but against the baptism of children, probably from six to ten years old. And a word more. In what *is* quoted here, there seems a little light to show Cramp is misleading. Tertullian says of the children he speaks of, " Why should this *innocent age* hasten to the remission of sins ?" Does not that look like an earlier age, as contemplated, than six or ten years ? Would six or ten years be regarded as not requiring forgiveness—innocent ? Again, why advise delay of *their* baptism, on the ground that such an age was incapable of learning about and knowing Christ ?

4

Let us next take the Baptist writer, Pengilly. He gives a larger extract from Tertullian—first in the Latin, and then a translation of it (in pp. 65, 66). I will quote you his translation. "The delay of baptism may be more advantageous, either on account of the condition, disposition, or age of ANY person, especially in reference to little children. For what necessity is there that the sponsors should be brought into danger? because either they themselves may fail of the promises by death, or be deceived by the growth of evil dispositions. The Lord, indeed, says, *Do not forbid them to come to me.* Let them, therefore, come when they are grown up; when they are taught whither they are to come. Let them become Christians when they can know Christ. Why should this innocent age hasten to the remission of sins? Men act more cautiously in worldly things; so that Divine things are here intrusted with whom earthly things are not. Let them know how to seek salvation, that you may appear to give to one that asketh. If persons understand the importance of baptism, they will rather fear the consequent obligation than the delay: true faith alone is secure of salvation."

Observe in the foregoing, Pengilly's translation indicates the age of the children in question. He calls them, not "children," as Cramp in his History, but "LITTLE children;" which does not correspond with "*not infants*, but children, probably from six to ten years of age." Again, the Latin word which he so translates "little children" is seen in his Latin extract (p. 65, first sentence), and is "parvulos." Now, anyone acquainted with Latin knows that *parvus* signifies "little," and that "parvulos" is the diminutive of *parvus*, and signifies "*very* little." On this let me cite you Pengilly in page 71, note at bottom, on another Latin passage. He gives it thus:—"Quicunque negat PARVULOS per baptismum Christi a perditione liberari," etc., which he translates himself thus:—"Whoever denies that INFANTS are, by Christian baptism, delivered from perdition," etc. Here he correctly renders "parvulos" by "infants," and "parvulos" is the word in Tertullian. What will we think of Cramp now and of his assertions, "Is it not obvious?" "It is quite clear, not infants, but children from six to ten years." Again, *Tertullian* there quotes from the New Testament to indicate the age of the children he referred to, viz., where our Lord says, "Do not forbid them to come unto me." Mark and Luke relate, and both describe, the same incident. In Mark (x. 13–16), Jesus is said to have " *taken them up in His arms* and blessed them," and they are called "little chil-. dren." He did not surely take up in His arms children of six or ten years. Of Luke (xviii. 15–17) I read in the *Baptist* version, "And they brought to Him also INFANTS that He might touch them," etc. It is "infants" there as in our version. Tertullian, therefore, by his quoting that passage plainly indicates it was to such he was referring. Further, Pengilly says, page 66, " INFANT baptism is first MENTIONED in the Christian Father (Tertullian) above quoted." " Tertullian opposes and reasons against INFANT baptism." J. Torrey Smith, on inside of Pengilly's book cover, admits the same.

Yet, once more from Cramp in his Catechism, now, on this point (p. 21), he asks, "Did Tertullian not refer to the baptism of LITTLE children?" He answers, "HE DID, but not with approval." So he allows now it was "little children, which he denies in his "History." He then gives Tertullian's words the same as in Pengilly, except the last two sentences there he omits. Yet, after all, at the bottom of the *same* page he remarks, "It was not a question of infant-baptism." "Tertullian referred to children" [he here drops out the term "little" admitted before]—to children—" probably from six to ten years of age."

Yes, brethren, and this is the leading standard historian of the Baptist Church, of whom Dr. Angus, Professor of Baptist College, Regent's Park, London, Eng., says in the preface of Dr. Cramp's Baptist History, " Dr. Cramp's candour and intelligence * * * have won the esteem and affection of all who know him. The reader will find a fuller and more satisfactory account in these pages than anywhere besides," etc. Well, I have no pleasure in the opposite of commendation. It is unpleasant to me; but I must say, after twice perusing the same history, I find it literally full of misrepresentation and special pleading such as we see here in Tertullian's case, and frequently contradictory in matters of fact, induced by the exigencies of the aim in view.

As I stated before, he states (p. 19 of his History), as the occasion of Tertullian's opposition to children's baptism, viz., "*Some* persons had *introduced* children (not *infants*) to baptism, OR *advocated* the administration of the ordinance to them." Now, neither he nor Pengilly, nor any others have pointed to one statement of Tertullian's to that effect, or the shadow of one, nor could they. He throughout speaks distinctly on the practice as the prevailing practice, and says not one word of it as an innovation, which you would expect he surely would, were it so. But on this here are their arguments. Weigh them :—Pengilly, p. 66, says,—" Tertullian opposes and reasons against infant-baptism as something unknown in the age of Christ and the apostles, and destitute of their authority, for WITH HIM their authority would not have been questioned FOR A MOMENT." After this, surely, now, the confiding reader will understand him to have been sound and most zealously obedient to the true faith, and a bulwark like another Paul, in the church, to all that was good and true. Yes, and yet Pengilly knew he became a very remarkable heresiarch, a follower and advocate of the man in his day, viz., Montanus, who gave himself out as the Holy Ghost incarnate. And Cramp, to magnify the force of his opposition to infant baptism, says, Catechism, p. 22, "If infant-baptism had been regarded as the law of Christ, Tertullian would not have DARED to advise its omission." Quite so. Now, it is the people also, who, at that time, were so very faithful to Scripture and Christ that no one would venture to teach or advise anything contrary thereto. Yet, besides Cramp's knowledge of Tertullian's Montanism, I have already quoted to you his description of his great unscripturalness on this same question of baptism in other more important aspects, to which let me add more from pp. 16–17 of his History, He gives there a description of "the development (in Tertullian's time) of those corrupting influences which had been at work," he says, "from the apostolic age, silently sapping the foundations of personal piety." "Instead of directing inquirers to the Atonement, and encouraging them to seek by prayer for the teaching and aid of the Holy Spirit, *the religious instructions of that age* expatiated on the vast powers of baptism. Tertullian, for example, declares," etc., (as quoted before in page 45.). He then continued—"When such opinions as these were entertained *is it not evident* that the door *was open* to manifold abuses," etc. Then, p. 19—"We have mentioned these particulars for the purpose of showing that at the beginning of the third century, religious declension had considerably advanced." And he adds, "*No one will now be surprised* at hearing that an attempt was made to extend the administration of baptism in an unwarrantable manner." The last sentence shows why Cramp exhibited the prevalence of corruption among the people and their teachings, Tertullian included. But, in a little, when the aim is to make out that Tertullian's opposition to infant-baptism was Scriptural, it is then maintained that the same people were so incorrupted and faithful to Scripture that he "would not have dared" to advise them not to baptize their little ones, were it Christ's will that they should be baptized. Consequently, since he did dare to advise them so, he was Scriptural, with an approving and truly pious people, very sound in the faith at his back. But there is one other aspect of Tertullian's treatise. In Pengilly's translation of his Latin extract, this is the first sentence, "The delay of baptism may be more advantageous, either on account of the *condition, disposition* or age of ANY persons, especially in reference to little children." Now, here is a reference to the propriety of delay in *others* besides little children. So little, however, of what Tertullian says on that subject is given by Baptist writers that readers don't perceive its force and bearing. I have shown you from Miller's Treatise, from Schaff and Hagenbach, (see pages 47 and 48) what all historians concur in testifying, and what I have read in Tertullian's treatise myself, that he advocated the delay of baptism by grown-up people, such as were unmarried—single men and women, widows and widowers—and as advisable, on the whole, to all till about to die. This being so—and Cramp, Pengilly, etc., knew it was—I now ask, Was this the law of Christ and His apostles, namely, that men and women converted from Judaism and heathenism should not be baptized as soon as they became believers, especially if they were single or widowed; but should defer it for years, or till death? Or does the *Baptist Church* act on this principle? What is the answer to each of these questions? No; NO. But

Tertullian did so advise and teach. Yet, Pengilly says, "With him the authority of Christ and his apostles would not be questioned for a moment," I am sure he did not learn that doctrine from their word or example, and his opposition to infant-baptism was of the same nature and based on reasons of precisely the same kind as his opposition to that of those grown-up in years. Although able and influential, in the human sense, his mind was dark, weak, and superstitious, religiously (Cramp's Hist., pp. 16–19), and, very unscripturally believing that sins after baptism probably incurred eternal condemnation, and excluded forever from the communion of the Church, he taught that all ages should consult their safety by deferring it till the deathbed, and some of all ages, more especially, as more liable to such danger.

We have now seen distinctly from his testimony, apart from his own opinions and conduct, that infant-baptism—with that of people of all ages when they embraced Christianity—was the prevailing practice of his day. Before proceeding further let us now take a summary view of the ground we have traversed.

It is admitted by all that John the Apostle received his Revelations in Patmos in A.D. 96, and died A.D. 100. Justin Martyr wrote his "Apology to the Emperor," etc., in A.D. 140 (Pengilly, p. 74.) He was then, and for some time previous, a leader of the Christians. When converted from heathenism (which was in A.D. 132) he had been a public teacher of philosophy, and was, therefore, we may presume, not less then than thirty years of age, and about forty when he wrote his Apology. Hence he must have been himself born about the time of the apostle John's death. Again, he was put to death A.D. 166, and Irenæus became a bishop A.D. 177 (Cramp' Hist., p. 18), that is, eleven years after Justin's martyrdom. But to become a *bishop* implied that he was then not much less than thirty years of age, whatever more. He would, therefore, have been Justin's cotemporary in life for about twenty years before Justin's death. Again, Irenæus died (Cramp's Hist., p. 18) in A.D. 202, and Tertullian wrote his treatise on Baptism (Cramp's Hist., p. 17) in A.D. 200; that is, Irenæus was alive then, and for two years after. Also, it is admitted by all that Tertullian was born about A.D. 160; he was, therefore, six years of age at Justin Martyr's death, and living at the same time as Irenæus for forty-two years, and outlived the latter, (Cramp's Hist., p. 17) from A.D. 202 to 220. Tertullian was, therefore, long a cotemporary of Irenæus, who, again, was of Justin, and Justin almost, if not literally, one of John the Apostle.

Again, Justin wrote in A.D. 140, in his "Apology," as we have seen—"MANY men and MANY women, SIXTY and SEVENTY years old, who, from children, have been *disciples* of Christ, preserve their continence." It may, of course, be added, legitimately, that *many* others who did not preserve their continence, but entered the marriage state, were also disciples from childhood. That is to say, there were MULTITUDES sixty and seventy years old when Justin wrote, who had been disciples from childhood. But sixty or seventy years from A.D. 140, would place the date of their childhood at A.D. 80 and 70, that is, twenty or thirty years *before* the end of the apostolic age, and but a few years after A.D. 64, 65, 66, when (as you will see in your Reference Bibles) the Epistles of Paul to the Ephesians, Philippians, Colossians, Timothy, Titus, Philemon and the Hebrews, and Peter's second epistle were written; and twenty years *before* the Revelation of John. And discipleship we showed was acknowledged then, as now, only of the baptized; with this difference—which makes the case the stronger—that they maintained that baptism effects regeneration, without which there is no real discipleship and by which there is. Here then is one complete and strong link of the chain of historical evidence on the observance of infant-baptism, reaching far into the apostolic age itself to a period long before the last surviving apostle had ceased his heaven inspired superintendence, and from thence to the time Justin wrote. Next, Irenæus, who became a bishop only eleven years after Justin's death —we have seen him distinctly affirm that people of all ages, and among these, "infants were regenerated unto God," and as distinctly affirm "that regeneration was effected by baptism, as Justin Martyr did before him." This second link clearly reaches within and embraces the first, and is of equally strong material to stand any candid and truth loving test. Then lastly, meanwhile, is the clear evidence in Tertullian, so long a cotemporary of the same time as

Irenæus with some years after. We have here then, a chain of three unbroken links, from full twenty years before the end of the apostolic age, till A.D. 200. And the evidence contained in them which I have set before you, remember, brethren, I have taken out of Baptist books, point by point, which of course settles the accuracy of the facts reasoned from, as beyond question from Baptists. I might have added more details, from other sources (as reliable of course as Baptist admissions) did my present object require it.

The next witness in the order of time is ORIGEN,—one of the most prolific and celebrated writers and teachers of the whole early Christian Church. Hagenbach, in his "Hist. of Doctrines," (vol. I. p. 194,) now open before me, remarks—"But it is worthy of notice that Origen in his commentary on the Epistle to the Romans chap. v. calls infant-baptism *a rite derived from the Apostles.*" Schaff (Hist. of the Christian Church vol. I. p. 403, now before me) says:—"Origen distinctly derives infant-baptism from the apostles; and *he himself*, being descended from Christian parents and grand-parents, *was baptized soon after his birth in* A.D. 185, and, through his journeys in the east and the west, was well acquainted with the practice of the Church in his time." Let us now hear Dr. Cramp's History. "Some writers," he says, p. 20, "have laboured hard to prove that Origen referred to infant-baptism as a then existing fact, and that he assigned to it an apostolic origin. Origen was the most learned man of that age. He flourished [that is, he wrote and taught] from A.D. 203 to A.D. 254, and attained high repute, both as a teacher in the catechetical school of Alexandria and as an author. But his references [mark this] are to *child* baptism, NOT to *infant*-baptism; and the difference between him and Tertullian is, that the latter decidedly objected to the *practice*, while Origen spoke of it with *approbation*." He next gives one quotation from Origen's reply to Celsus, a heathen writer, which does not bear directly on the question, and then dismisses Origen from his History, without presenting to his readers that they might judge for themselves the clear and telling passages Origen did write, which I will now show you, yes, and in the first place from Cramp's own Catechism. Of course thousands who have read and will read his History will not read his Catechism, a separate book. In it (p. 28) he asks,—"Is it not affirmed that Origen argued in favour of infant-baptism?" He first answers by a disingenuous attempt to get rid of the passages he is about to quote by insinuating that *they may have been* altered by translators in an unwarrantable manner, when no Baptist or any other has undertaken to show that such has been the case of them; but which are admitted by all honourable writers to be as genuine and authentic as any we have. He then remarks:—" In the passages which refer to baptism . . . Origen says that '*infants* are baptized for the remission of sins,' and that 'by the sacrament of baptism the pollution of *birth* is taken away.' In one place he observes that baptism is administered ' even to little children, according to the usage of the Church,' and in another, that 'the Church has received from the apostles a tradition to give baptism even to little children.'" I note here, for after use, that Cramp does not specify the places in or names of Origen's works where these passages occur.

Now, remember that Cramp says *in his History*, as I quoted to you, that " Origen's references were to *child* baptism, NOT to *infant*-baptism," and does not give his readers one of the passages, but leaves them to take his word for it. And why not? Are they not told by the Baptist Professor, Dr. Angus, in the Introductory Notice at the beginning of the History, that Dr. Cramp's candour, intelligence, etc., have won him the esteem of *all* who know him. *These* qualities will be found to distinguish the volume," etc. Alas! What do you think, brethren? Look again at those passages where he actually, in his Catechism, states it WAS *infant*-baptism Origen spoke of, "with approbation," and AS a then existing fact, practised, too, from the apostles' time, and as taking away the pollution of BIRTH.

However, we must hear Cramp out. After giving those passages, he remarks: " Now, this is not the style of a man who knew that he could adduce, ' Thus saith the Lord' in confirmation of his statements. He would not have appealed to 'the usage of the Church,' or spoken so vaguely of 'a tradition,' if he could have said as was the practice of early Christian authors, ' It is written.' Why did he not say *where* the tradition was to be found? He knew that it was *only* a tradition, and that neither precept nor precedent had been discovered in the New Testament." This is special pleading in earnest—that will satisfy an already biased Baptist reader and mislead others no doubt, as thistle seeds will take root, and subtle sophistries will deceive. Now observe, *each* of these passages of Origen occur in his expositions of *Scripture*, which Cramp knew, but kept silent on it. How then could his readers know that? He was bringing out the meaning and truth of what was 'written' and what 'saith the Lord' and enforcing *that* by reference to baptism. But, even the passages Cramp gives, *he gives in a mangled form*, as meagre, by suppressing portions as would leave room to carp and distort the meaning.

Let me now give them to you from Miller's Treatise, p. 23 :—" To say nothing of earlier intimations, wholly irreconcilable with any other practice than that of infant-baptism, Origen, a Greek Father of the third century, and decidedly the most learned man of his day, speaks in the most unequivocal terms of the baptism of infants, as the general practice of the Church in his time, and as having been received from the apostles. His testimony is as follows :—' According to the usage of the Church, baptism is given even to infants ; when, if there were nothing in infants which needed forgiveness and mercy, the grace of baptism would seem to be superfluous.' (Homil. viii. in Levit., ch. 12). Again, 'Infants are baptized for the forgiveness of sins. Of what sins? Or, when have they sinned? Or, can there be any reason for the laver in their case, unless it be according to the sense which we have mentioned above, viz.: that no one is free from pollution, though he has lived but one day upon earth. And, because, by baptism native pollution is taken away, therefore infants are baptized.' (Homil. in Luc. 14). Again, 'For this cause it was that the church received an order from the apostles to give baptism even to infants.' (Comment. in Epist. ad Romanos Lib. 5)." Note in the last sentence here the words "received an order for." Cramp, as before shown, says instead " received a tradition."

You will now be able, brethren, I doubt not, to see that Origen's testimony is as clear as to the fact of infant-baptism having been observed from the apostles' time, as clear can be. He was himself born only eighty-five years after the death of the apostle John, so that the preceding time was short to which he bore witness, and in the case of such a writer and teacher, who stated those things to the people living then, who themselves knew something of the *facts*, his testimony alone would be enough. But we have given you more than his.

But what says Pengilly on this subject? He professes, of course, to be honest and candid, though we have found him erring very seriously notwithstanding, and inexcusably so. Well, in pp. 65-67 of his " Scripture Guide to Baptism," he professes to be giving the evidence of its early church history as to infants. .He passes over Justin Martyr and Irenæus as if they had never written a word about infants being regenerated to God, and that effected by baptism; nor about multitudes being disciples from childhood. His first name is Tertullian, and his *next* Cyprian, and so on after. But Origen, who was between Tertullian and Cyprian, is not as much as mentioned there at all. And his was no obscure name, but greater far than Tertullian's, nor were his utterances on baptism obscure or of no value in the controversy, as you have just seen. I suppose the secret is, the less said about him the better for the Baptist cause. At any rate, Pengilly, in his list in those pages, does not so much as mention his name. But in one other part of his book he does. Let us see what he says. In page 70 he asks, "Who is the *first* Christian writer that defended the baptism of infants? Answer— The first that mentioned the practice at all was Tertullian, A.D. 204. It was named next by Origen, A.D. 280. But the first writer that *defended* the practice was Cyprian, A.D. 253." This is literally ALL that Pengilly says about Origen throughout in the matter:—"It was NAMED next by Origen." Now, brethren, you have seen even from Cramp's Catechism (not his History; it would not do to be there either), the direct and clear testimony that Origen gave, and you have seen it from Hagenbach, Schaff, and Miller, and can judge whether he only just *named* it, and might not well be said to have *defended* it, too, as well as Cyprian, who followed; and to have spoken of the church and apostles as more than naming it, too, but ordering, practising it. That, however, is all Pengilly can be got to say, *though* HE KNEW OTHERWISE, *but* WOULD NOT DIVULGE THE PARTICULARS. In these ways, with their candour (!) and commendations of each other they mislead, deceive, the ignorant and confiding.

I will conclude this section with one or two remarkable quotations from Baptist writers that may surprise you, brethren, though probably not now. The book of Dr. Geo. B. Taylor, published by the Philadelphia Baptist Publication Society, which I quoted from once before, entitled "The Baptists: Who they are, and, What they have Done," says, p. 31, " During the first TWO AND A HALF centuries, WE CLAIM that NO TRACES of the EXISTENCE of INFANT baptism are to be found." Cramp's Catechism, p. 48, " Cyprian was the FIRST Christian writer on behalf of infant-baptism." Now the date of his writing, as we shall see presently, was A.D. 253, or two and a half centuries after the birth of Christ, and twenty-three years after Origen wrote on it. Again, p. 24, " Observe, MORE THAN two hundred years passed away after the *establishment* of the Christian church, *before infant-baptism made its appearance*." But the Christian church was not begun to be established till after Jesus ascended to heaven, A.D. thirty-four. So, *more than* 200 years after that brings us to A.D. 253. Cramp's History, p. 29, " Paedobaptism, meaning thereby the baptism of new-born infants, with the vicarious promises of parents and other sponsors, was UTTERLY UNKNOWN to the early church, not only down to the end of the second, but, indeed, to the *middle* of the *third* century." The middle of the third century was A.D. 250.

As to "sponsors," Pengilly, p. 66, translates Tertullian on infant-baptism, as saying, "For what necessity is there that the sponsors should be brought into danger, etc.? *Cramp* also, in his Catechism, p. 21, (but nothing in his History of this), gives the *same* translation as correct. Now, in these quoted assertions, by a stroke of the pen, (and a stout heart) all evidence of the contrary is obliterated to and from their readers, and this is published by the Baptist Church of America, Canada, etc., in many thousands of copies, and repeated from these books, under such authority, by many more thousands of lips continually. So it seems in Origen, who wrote his NAMING of infant-baptism in A.D. 230, according to Pengilly, p. 70; in Tertullian, A.D. 200, and in Irenæus, and Justin Martyr, A.D. 177, 140, there is not even "a trace." of infant-baptism. It was "utterly unknown" in their days! Such, brethren, is the "truthfulness, soberness, and impartiality" of Cramp, and of that Dr. Taylor who was so much impressed with the evidence of these qualities in Cramp. And such is the way the Baptist Church makes out the evidence of history to establish (!) its tenets. "By their fruits ye shall know them."

But, however much they may by such policy, try to blind the people as to the facts and truth, and succeed too, alas; we have the evidence before us to judge from it for ourselves; which you observe I have set before you and substantiated even from Baptist admissions, however reluctantly made. Origen, therefore, is another complete link in the unbroken chain of evidence. and a very strong one with a clear ring, embracing those links preceding and embraced in turn by the next now to be glanced at, namely:—

CYPRIAN.—On the evidence from him, and the others in council with him on the occasion, I will first read you from Miller, p. 23:—" In the year 253 after Christ there was a Council of sixty-six bishops or pastors, held at Carthage, in which Cyprian presided. To this Council, *Fidus*, a country pastor, presented the following question, which he wished them, by their united wisdom, to solve, viz., Whether it was necessary, in the administration of baptism, as of circumcision, to wait until the *eigthth* day; or whether a child might be baptized at an earlier period after its birth? The question, it will be observed, was *not* whether infants ought to be baptized? *That* was taken for granted. But simply, whether it was necessary to wait until the *eighth* day after their birth? The Council came UNANIMOUSLY to the following decision, and transmitted it in a letter to the inquirer (as follows):—' Cyprian, and the rest of the bishops who were present in the Council, sixty-six in number, to Fidus, our brother, greeting, As to the case of infants—whereas you judge that they must not be baptized within two or three days after they are born, and that the rule of circumcision is to be observed, that no one should be baptized and sanctified before the eighth day after he is born; we were, ALL in the Council, of a very different opinion. As for what you thought proper to be done, no one was of your mind; but we all rather judged that the mercy and grace of God is to be denied to no human being that is born. This, therefore, dear brother, was our opinion in the Council: that we ought not to hinder any person from baptism, and the grace of God, who is merciful and kind to us all. And this rule, as it holds for all, we think more especially to be observed in reference to infants, even to those newly-born.' (Cyprian, Epist. 66). Surely no testimony (continues Miller) can be more unexceptionable and decisive than this. Lord Chancellor King, in his account of the Primitive church, after quoting what is given above, subjoins the following remark :—' Here, then, is a synodical decree for the baptism of infants, as formal as can possibly be expected; which being the judgment of a synod, is more authentic and cogent than that of a private father; it being supposable that a private father might write his own particular judgment and opinion only; but the determination of a synod (and he might have added, the *unanimous* determination of a synod of sixty-six members) denotes the common practice and usage of the whole church.' "

Cramp, feeling disposed now to acknowledge infant-baptism, explains this case in his Catechism, p. 24, in accordance with what I have given you from Miller, and then makes a remarkable addition. He says, "Besides, Cyprian added, as the mercy of God should be withheld from none who sought it, there was a special reason for bestowing it on new-born infants, inasmuch as *they*, as soon as they enter into the world, *manifest*, by their loud cries and tears, *their earnest desire for the blessing.*" It is noteworthy of this, however, that giving it without quotation commas, and in indirect narration, he professes merely to give an account in his own words, not Cyprian's, of what Cyprian said. Of course it is expected at the same time that his account is a correct one. It implies clearly that Cyprian, and the sixty-six bishops, in whose name he wrote, believed and taught that new-born infants (or men) are not, by nature, depraved and at enmity with God and the things of His Spirit, but as soon as born they show a very different and good spirit in that they 'manifest an earnest desire for the blessing of God's grace and salvation'—which is a doctrine most vitally at variance with the truth and plain teachings of Scripture. Cramp in his *History*, however, gives a large extract (pp. 23, 24) from the letter in question of Cyprian, but neither there nor anywhere else in his history does any mention of this nature appear. But what, in his Catechism, he evidently refers to, I find in Pengilly in page 67, as follows:—" Cyprian, A.D. 253. ' As far as lies in us, no soul, if possible, is to be lost. It is not for us to hinder any person from baptism and the grace of God; which rule, as it holds to all, so we think it more especially to be observed in reference to infants, to whom our help and the Divine mercy is rather to be granted; because, by their weeping and wailing at their first entrance into the world, they do intimate nothing so much as that they *implore compassion*." Now that these are Cyprian's *own words* is attested by the Baptist writer, Pengilly, who ends his quotation of them as here.

And, looking at their meaning, Dr. Cramp's account is very different, indeed; and did he, or would anyone, not perceive that? To say that 'new-born infants by their weeping, etc., intimate that they implore compassion,' is surely not the same as to say that 'by it they manifest their earnest desire for the blessing' of God. When an infant weeps (which does indeed successfully appeal to our pity) do we understand it from that to be earnestly desiring the blessings of salvation. Yet such is the interpretation of Cramp in regard to these words of Cyprian, while he withholds from his readers Cyprian's words, who are led, therefore, to believe that he and the Council actually taught that doctrine. Yet, in his History, p. 24, I find the following statement given as Cyprian's in the very letter in question—" the child just born has brought with it, by its descent from Adam, the infection of the old death." How differently this sounds, and how Scriptural? But, because he and the Council were manifestly Paedobaptists, Cramp endeavours to weaken the historic evidence by making them ridiculous, with evidence before him to the contrary, and by garbled representation of his own manipulation.

As the evidence of this Council of Carthage, as thoroughly indicating the doctrine and practice of infant-baptism, cannot be gainsaid, the Baptist policy is to belittle it.

They try to make believe that infant-baptism was then practised in that part of the world only, and that the practice did not extend elsewhere till long after. In this they completely ignore, as if a word of it had never been written or seen, all the testimony I have shown you, even out of Baptist books when discussing the places, and from other sources, of Origen and Tertullian, of Irenæus, and Justin Martyr, and the others to be added. It is true, some of them, as Pengilly and J. Torrey Smith, admit the existence of *infant*-baptism in Tertullian's time, who wrote on it fifty-three years prior to that Council of Carthage. Yet others, as I have before shown you (p. 60) don't scruple to " claim that no traces of the existence of infant-baptism are to be found during the first two and a half centuries;" that it " was introduced at the middle of the third century," and was " utterly unknown " till then. The books that contain such strong unscrupulous language, as Cramp's History, and Taylor's, before specified, etc., are careful not to supply their readers with the evidence that does exist to the contrary.

In his *Catechism*, however, p. 25, Cramp, besides *its* other admissions concedes a little more, namely, " The utmost that can be affirmed is, that infant-baptism had grown up into a practice in Northern Africa [where Carthage was] about the middle of the third century." Well, as it evidently was in universal practice at the time of the Council, it would have taken a considerable time before it grew up to its dimensions then. So here is evidence itself that long before A.D. 253 it had existence. But he adds, " *There is no evidence respecting its existence at that time in any other part of the world.*" This sentence he puts in italics to show the importance he wishes to attach to it.

Of the Christian writers we have examined besides Cyprian, Origen's testimony cannot be said to refer to Carthage in particular, as he did not reside near it ; but for most part in Alexandria (Cramp's Hist., p. 20), and had travelled much, residing for a time, and writing diligently, at Palestine, Rome, and other places. It was in Rome where, among other things, he prepared his famous " Hexapla " of the Bible in six different languages. Also what he says so fully and repeatedly on infant-baptism, he speaks of it not in relation to any particular district, but of the Church at large. (See his words again, p. 58) " Tertullian," as Cramp informs us (Hist., p. 16), " was a native of Carthage, in Africa, and spent most of his life in that city." Irenæus was a native of Greece, and a bishop in Lyons, France. And Justin Martyr was a native of Palestine, travelled much, but spent the best part of his life at Rome, where he wrote his 'Apology,' and suffered martyrdom. So, brethren, if I have furnished you with evidence of the existence of infant-baptism in their days, its existence will then be seen to have been all over the Christian world. Besides, the fact that it was universally practised by the church when Origen wrote (not to mention just now that he testified to its derivation from the apostles), implies necessarily its existence long before then, as such prevalence could not take place all at once among many thousands and millions of people. The same reasoning applies to Tertullian's testimony and to Irenæus's and Justin's.. Also Origen, a native of Alexandria, in A.D. 185, it appears, was himself baptized in infancy (p. 56).

But suppose, as Cramp affirms, no evidence were now available of its existence in any other part of the world than at Carthage and vicinity, would that be *proof* that it *did not* exist elsewhere ? They affirm, emphatically, Yes ; for they affirm everything with emphasis, even the grossest misrepresentations. Well, let us see. And in the first place, I affirm this, and what is often affirmed, and no Baptist can prove untrue, what while many writers of those early ages have testified of the prevalence over the Church of infant-baptism, and written of and administered it as the ordinance of Christ, of Scripture, and apostolic practice, there is but one writer during the first eleven hundred years A.D. who can be shown to have opposed it, namely, Tertullian ; and he opposed it in adults for the same reasons as in infants, and these reasons admittedly very unscriptural. Next, it is held by us in regard to the Sabbath Day, for example, that it was kept sacred by the people of God, according to the divine command, from our first parents' time on to that of Moses. Yet, in all the book of Genesis, containing the history of men for more than 2,000 years, its observance in practice is not once mentioned. Is silence on the subject, then, a proof of its violation all that time and by the great and good men of that period, and notwithstanding its being set apart and hallowed for observance by God at the creation? (Genesis, chap. ii, 2, 3). Again, we know for certain of the universal prevalence of infant-baptism in Northern Africa at the time in question. The Baptists admit this fully. BUT HOW DO WE KNOW THIS LARGE AND INDISPUTABLE FACT? Notice this, brethren. The only reason why we have the knowledge of it from the Council of Carthage in Cyprian's letter, was a mere incident that easily might not have occurred, viz., *Fidus*, a country bishop or pastor, had a difficulty in his mind as to "whether (to take Pengilly's statement of it, p. 70, note) an infant, before it was eight days old, might be baptized, if need required." He had doubts for certain reasons, and "thought it best, therefore (Cramp's Hist., p. 23), to wait till the eighth day, and to baptize the infant at the same time, at which, under the law, it would have been circumcised. But he asked advice of Cyprian (by letter), who laid the case before a council, which had assembled at Carthage in the year 252 [Pengilly, Miller, etc., say A.D. 253] for the settlement of *various ecclesiastical matters*. Sixty-six bishops met on that occasion. The answer is given in a letter written by Cyprian." This, then, was the sole occasion of the matter being before the Council at all. It was assembled for other matters. And the fact that all the bishops or pastors, without exception, were of the mind, different from the scruples of Fidus, that it was not necessary to wait till the eighth day, shows that the great majority of the pastors *of the Church* would not have Fidus's difficulty. Now, *but for this simple occurrence we would have no historical evidence from that Council about infant-baptism at all.* Had he then not had those doubts, he would not have asked advice on them, the Council would not have had occasion to consider them, nor Cyprian to write him on the subject. And consequently there would be no evidence from it or Cyprian on the subject of infant-baptism at all. And what then would our Baptist friends say according to their mode of argument? They would affirm that the Church in North Africa *did not* administer baptism to infants at all. Yet, it is plain, the Council did not institute the baptism of infants, but that that practice was prevalent in all the congregations long before it assembled, Fidus himself administering it as well as the rest. This was the widespread fact, and would have been the same independently of the Council and Fidus, suppose the one and the other had never been heard of. Consequently the absence of historical evidence as to other places, especially at so remote and unfavourable a period, would not prove its non-existence there. Of its prevalence elsewhere, throughout the church at large, I have, however, given you ample proof from other sources; to which I will add quite a galaxy, and then close.

I have now unfolded to your view, brethren, another well-established link in the historical chain, and of good material, that links well into the four preceding, the first of which embraces firmly many years of the apostolic age. Origen, the last of the preceding four witnesses, died (Cramp's Hist., p. 20), in A.D. 254; and Cyprian, with his sixty-six brethren, unanimously testified A.D. 253; or, according to Cramp, A.D. 252—that is, one or two years before Origen was called to rest from his manifold labours; their evidence comprehending necessarily a long period prior to the date of the Council.

I have not much more now to do, but what I have to present is of much value on the subject of inquiry. From the different reasons mentioned at the beginning, the writings on this, as on other questions, are fewer the further the period is away from us, and during the times that the Imperial Governments were heathen and actively hostile to Christianity; still the Lord in His providence has preserved and handed down to us sufficiently full and clear testimony on this line of inquiry.

You will remember, remarkable as it is, that Cramp affirms that the first instance of the existence of infant-baptism does not appear till the Council of Carthage, A.D. 253. Well, in his Catechism, p. 26, he puts the question, "How soon after the first instance of infant-baptism recorded in history did it come into general observance?" He answers :—" Not for several centuries." I will now briefly show you that this, like *so many* other of his sayings, is as gross a misstatement of fact as, in the circumstances, could be penned. The expression, "*several* centuries" will always be understood by his readers to mean more than two—at the very least three, and more likely four or five centuries. Suppose, then, we add *only three* centuries to A.D. 253, they would bring us so A.D. 553, as the time before which the baptism of infants was not *generally* observed, that is, the middle of the SIXTH century.

On this part of the subject I will read you at length from Dr. Miller's Treatise (p. 24–28). He there says:— "The famous CHRYSOSTOM, a Greek father, who flourished toward the close *of the* FOURTH century, having had occasion to speak of circumcision, and of the inconvenience and pain which attended its dispensation, proceeds to say: 'But *our* circumcision, I mean the grace of baptism, gives cure without pain, and procures to us a thousand benefits, and fills us with the grace of the Spirit; and it has *no determinate time* as that had; but one that is in the *very beginning of his age*, or one that is in the middle of it, or one that is in his old age, may receive this circumcision made without hands; in which there is no trouble to be undergone but to throw off the load of sins, and to receive pardon for all past offences' (Homil. 40, in Genesin).

"Passing by the testimony of several other conspicuous writers of the THIRD and FOURTH centuries, in support of the fact, that infant-baptism was GENERALLY PRACTISED when they wrote, I shall detain you with only one testimony more in relation to the history of this ordinance. It is that of AUGUSTINE, one of the most pious, learned and venerable fathers of the Christian Church, who lived *a little more than three hundred years after the apostles*—taken in connection with that of *Pelagius*, the learned heretic, who lived at the same time. Augustine had been pleading against Pelagius, in favour of the doctrine of original sin. In the course of this plea he asks, "Why are infants baptized for the remission of sins, if they have no sins?" At the same time intimating to Pelagius, that if he would be consistent with himself, his denial of original sin must draw after it the denial of infant-baptism. The reply of Pelagius is striking and unequivocal. 'Baptism,' says he, 'ought to be administered to infants with the same sacramental words which are used in the case of adult persons.' 'Men slander me as if I denied the sacrament of baptism to infants.' 'I NEVER HEARD OF ANY, *not even the most impious heretic, who denied baptism to infants*; for who can be so impious as to hinder infants from being baptized, and born again in Christ, and so make them miss of the kingdom of God.' Again, Augustine remarks in reference to the Pelagians :—' Since they grant that infants must be baptized, as not being able to *resist the authority of the whole Church, which was doubtless delivered by our Lord and His apostles,* they must consequently grant that they stand in need of the benefit of the Mediator ; that being offered by the sacrament, and by the charity [love] of the faithful, and so being incorporated into Christ's body, they may be reconciled to God,' etc. Again, speaking of certain heretics at Carthage, who, though they acknowledged infant-baptism, took wrong views of its meaning, Augustine remarks : —' They, *minding the Scriptures, and the authority of the whole Church,* and the form of the sacrament itself, see well that baptism in infants is for the remission of sins.' Further, in his work against the Donatists, the same writer, speaking of baptised infants obtaining salvation without the personal exercise of faith, he says :—' Which the *whole body of the Church holds,* as delivered to them in the case of little infants baptized, who certainly cannot believe with the heart unto righteousness, or confess with the mouth unto salvation, nay, by their crying and noise while the sacrament is administering, they disturb the holy mysteries ; and yet *no Christian 'man* will say that they are baptized to no purpose.' Again, he says :—' The custom of our mother the church in baptizing infants must not be disregarded, nor be accounted needless, nor believed to be anything else than *an ordinance delivered to us from the Apostles.'* In short, those who will be at the trouble to consult the large extracts from the writings of Augustine, among other Christian fathers, in the learned *Wall's* History of Infant-baptism, will find that venerable father declaring again and again that he never met with any Christian, either of the general church, or of any of the sects, nor with any writer, who owned the authority of Scripture, who taught any other doctrine than that infants were to be baptized for the remission of sin. Here, then, were two men, undoubtedly among the most learned men in the world—Augustine and Pelagius ; the former as familiar, probably, with the writings of all the distinguished fathers who had gone before him, as any man of his time ; the latter, also a man of great learning and talent, who had travelled over a great part of the Christian world; who both declare, about three hundred years after the apostolic age, that they never saw or heard of any one who called himself a Christian, not even the most impious heretic; no, nor any writer who claimed to believe in the Scriptures, who denied the baptism of infants. (See Wall's History, part I., ch. 15-19). Can the most incredulous reader, who is not fast bound in the fetters of invincible prejudice, hesitate to admit, first, that these men verily believe that infant-baptism had been the universal practice of the Church from the days of the apostles; and, secondly, that, situated and informed as they were, it was impossible that they should be mistaken.

"The same Augustine, in his *Epistle to Boniface*, while he expresses an opinion that the parents are the proper persons to offer up their children to God in baptism, if they be good, faithful Christians; yet thinks proper to mention that others may with propriety, in special cases, perform the same kind office of Christian charity. 'You see,' says he, 'that a great many are offered, not by their parents, but by any other persons, as infant slaves are sometimes offered by their masters. And sometimes when the parents are dead, the infants are baptized, being offered by any that can afford to show this compassion on them. And sometimes infants, whom their parents have cruelly exposed, may be taken up and offered in baptism by those who have no children of their own, nor design to have any.' Again, in his book against the Donatists, speaking directly of infant-baptism, he says:—'If any one ask for divine authority in this matter, although that which *the whole Church practises*, which *was not instituted by councils*, but was *ever in use*, is very reasonably believed to be no other than a thing delivered by the authority of the apostles; yet we may, besides, take a true estimate, how much the sacrament of baptism does avail infants by the circumcision which God's ancient people received. For Abraham was justified before he received circumcision, as Cornelius was endued with the Holy Spirit before he was baptized. And yet the apostles say of Abraham, that he received the sign of circumcision, ' a seal of the righteousness of faith,' by which he had in heart believed, and it had been 'counted to him for righteousness.' Why, then, was he commanded to circumcise all his male infants on the eighth day, when they could not yet believe with the heart, that it might be counted to them for righteousness; but for this reason, because the sacrament is, in itself, of great importance? Therefore, as in Abraham, 'the righteousness of faith' went before, and circumcision, the seal of the righteousness of faith, came after; so in Cornelius, the spiritual sanctification by the gift of the Holy Spirit went before, and the sacrament of regeneration, by the laver of baptism, came after. And as in Isaac, who was circumcised the eighth day, the seal of the righteousness of faith went before, and (as he was a follower of his father's faith) the righteousness itself, the seal whereof had gone before in his infancy, came after; so in infants baptized, the sacrament of regeneration goes before, and (if they put in practice the Christian religion) conversion of the heart, the mystery whereof went before in their body, comes after. By all which it appears, that the sacrament of baptism is one thing, and conversion of the heart another.'

"So much for the testimony of the Fathers. To me, I acknowledge, this testimony carries with it irresistible conviction. It is no doubt, conceivable, considered in itself, that in three centuries from the days of the apostles a very material change might have taken place in regard to the subjects of baptism. But that a change so serious and radical as that of which our Baptist friends speak, should have been introduced without the knowledge of such men as have been just quoted, is *not conceivable*. That the church should have passed from the practice of none but adult baptism, to that of the constant and universal baptism of infants, while such a change was utterly unknown, and never heard of, by the most active, pious, and learned men that lived during that period, cannot, I must believe, be imagined by any impartial mind. Now when Origen, Cyprian, and Chrysostom, declare, not only that the baptism of infants was the universal and unopposed practice of the church in their respective times and places of residence; and when men of so much acquaintance with all preceding writers, and so much knowledge of all Christendom, as Augustine and Pelagius, declared that they *never heard of any one who claimed to be a Christian, either orthodox or heretic, who did not maintain and practice infant baptism;* I say, to suppose, in the face of such testimony, that the practice of infant baptism crept in, as an unwarranted innovation, between their time and that of the apostles, without the smallest notice of the change having ever reached their ears is, I must be allowed to say, of all incredible suppositions, one of the most incredible. He who can believe this, must it appears to me, be prepared to make a sacrifice of all historical evidence at the shrine of blind and deaf prejudice," etc., etc.

After such complete and weighty testimony, brethren, you will be convinced, I presume that no further evidence on the subject of inquiry is required. While even Tertullian bore ample testimony to the prevalence of infant baptism in his early day, he was not himself an absolute opponent of it, as he admitted its propriety, and therefore its Scriptural authority, where there appeared the probability of death in infancy, and the same in regard to others of adult years. But in other cases preferred its delay as long as possible from his unscriptural ideas of the character and consequences of sins that might be committed after its administration as distinguished from the same if committed by the same persons if unbaptized.

In regard to the voluminous testimony I have just placed before you on the historical evidence of our subject, Baptist writers don't deny its authenticity or genuineness, its validity being beyond question; but the plan adopted with their readers is, to withhold it in silence as if no such testimony existed; and in some cases to give one or two short quotations of their own selection, not the strongest, you may be sure, and, presenting these as if that were all, to distort the author's meaning in that same, which could be perceived by their readers if more were given of what is unnoticed. In his History, which professes to deal fully with the subject, Cramp does not give A SINGLE WORD of the foregoing testimony. He merely remarks that Augustine was a powerful advocate of infant-baptism, affirming, by the way, that "his sheet anchor in the argument was the supposed efficacy of baptism in removing the defilement of original sin," (p. 31.) Of Chrysostom he gives no statement at all. But of Pelagius, *the great heretic*, he states something—that "he did not deny the propriety of baptizing infants, who obtained, he said, the 'kingdom of heaven by their baptism, which 'kingdom of heaven,' he distinguished from eternal life, and represented as a kind of intermediate state." And continues, "we need not dwell on such follies." He thus seeks to make the question ridiculous by identifying it with such an advocate, but he fails to hint in the smallest degree that as Pelagius had taught that infants had no original or other sin, Augustine accused his doctrine of drawing after it the rejection of infant-baptism by implication, and that his admission of the propriety of infant baptism was not spontaneous but because he did not wish to oppose what was everywhere acknowledged as scriptural and apostolic. Had Cramp, instead of giving Pelagius' opinions, or in addition, given a statement or two of his on the historical matter of *fact*, such as when he replied to Augustine, "I never heard of any, not even the most impious heretic, who denied baptism to infants," etc., and had further added, what all historians agree in testifying, that he was a very learned and widely travelled man, he would have done a little justice in the matter. But this he has refrained from. In his Catechism all he chooses to give from them, or any others of the fourth century, is two short passages from Augustine, (p. 28,) both contained in six lines, in one of which the expression "an ordinance delivered to us from the apostles," he makes into "a tradition of the apostles;" and exercises his ingenuity on the unsatisfactory nature of custom and tradition—of which ingenuity we have seen specimens before, in his treatment of Origen and Tertullian in regard to "not infant but child baptism," etc., etc.

You will recollect his assertion that "infant baptism did not come into *general* observance for several centuries" after the middle of the third century, (Catech. p. 24, 26,) that is, at the earliest, till the middle of the sixth. The testimony of the celebrated writers of the close of the FOURTH century on its general observance then, as well as from apostolic times, you have now seen; and are able therefore to see in another instance how opposed his statements are to the facts of history.

When the evidence of the history of our subject becomes overwhelming in its fulness, while the policy of the Baptist is, on the one hand, as we have said, to withhold that evidence, on the other hand they seek to weaken the force of what they cannot deny, by different expedients. One of these is strongly to represent the unsoundness of doctrine that prevailed on the effect of baptism. Well, granting that such was prevalent, and was so of other things as well; still the fact remains, independent of that, that the baptism of infants has been shewn to have been observed by the Church at large all along from the days of the apostles, and no complaint against it as an innovation contrary to Scripture and apostolic practice, but weighty testimony to the reverse of these. But the views held on the other sacrament, for example, the Lord's Supper, were certainly as far divergent from Scripture, as those on baptism; yet these are no proof against its Scriptural authority and apostolic observance. Of that there is no question. But our Baptist friends will say, Yes, but it is distinctly appointed in the Bible; and we say so too. Still the argument remains, therefore, indisputable that unsoundness of doctrine about an ordinance is no proof that the ordinance itself is not a scriptural one. The Jewish teachers in the time of our Saviour, and no doubt for ages before, spoke very extravagantly and unscripturally, among other things of the Sabbath day, yet that was no proof against its divine appointment. The fact that it can be proven from the 20th chap. of Exodus, etc., only decides the correctness of my argument. The abuse of things does not prove that those things themselves have no divine authority, and no proper place and use all along.

But, though my line of investigation at present, is into the early history of the Church, from and after the apostolic age, in demonstrating that infant-baptism is not a relic of the Popish church of Rome, yet we do not rest our case on the testimony of such evidence, serviceable as it is, in its sphere. The authority of our faith and practice in this, as in other things, is the Scriptures of the Old and New Testaments; from which we can prove infant, as well as adult baptism. I don't mean, however, that we can convince every one of this, any more than we can convince every one of the divinity of Jesus, or of the personality of the Holy Ghost, or of the immortality of the soul, the everlasting punishment of the wicked, the inheritance by our race of original sin, the total depravity of our nature, the substitutionary obedience and endurance of God's wrath and curse for sinners of mankind by Jesus Christ, justification by faith in Him alone ; or, in order to the indispensable requisites of "repentance towards God and faith in our Lord Jesus Christ," that there is an absolute necessity that the Holy Spirit supernaturally produce or create those conditions of mind in us ; or that the Lord's Supper is not the literal body and blood of Christ; or that the administration of baptism by water does not regenerate the soul of young or old, etc., etc., each of which, and more also, is refused as untrue by very many, who say they can't see them taught in Scripture.

But to return. While we affirm that all that Baptist writers aver on unsoundness of doctrine, does not affect the historical evidence of fact, there is reason to reply that they make those Christian writers often appear more unsound than they were ; just as Romish advocates extract from their writings, disconnectedly and unfairly, to make out their tenets Romish, where they were not. For instance, Cramp in his Catechism (p. 29), remarking on the participation by infants of the Lord's Supper, and after saying that "Augustine enforced it on the ground of its necessity to salvation, appealing to John vi. 53 ;" (but he neither gives Augustine's own words, nor states the place where they are to be seen, so that I cannot look them up to see if correctly given); he then continues :—"Gelasius, bishop of Rome, decreed (A.D. 495), that ' no one should venture to exclude any child from this sacrament (the Lord's Supper), without which no one can attain eternal life.' (*Hagenbach's History of Doctrines*, vol. I., p. 367)." Now I have this volume of Hagenbach's before me—precisely the same edition that Cramp had. In his History he quotes from the same volume twice (p. 7, 15), on another matter, and I have verified them in the same page and words as he there gives. But in the page, 367, referred to for Gelasius's decree, I find no mention of it or him. In the next page (368), which begins the section *on the Lord's Supper*, there is no such statement of him (or of any other) nor in the whole section, which I have minutely examined. But Hagenbach does state of him in that page, " Gelasius, bishop of Rome, *spoke very decidedly* against *the idea of a real change*" in the elements of bread and wine. Again he is referred to, to show this, in p. 372, by an extract from his writings, but there is nothing said there whatever of infant communion. Next I look into the index of this and the second volume, and find Gelasius' name with reference only to that place above explained; and lastly, I have carefully gone over vol. I. and also Vol. II., and seen no further trace of him, and am sure he is not even referred to more. So that that quotation of Cramp from Hagenbach is not to be found in Hagenbach in the place specified or elsewhere.

Another expedient is to draw atttention to some Christians of eminence in the church of the fourth century who though of Christian, (some of them of pious) parentage were not baptized till their manhood. In his Catechism (p. 27) Cramp specifies four cases of this kind, Ephrem of Edesse, Gregory Nazianzen, Basil of Cæsarea and Chrysostom. And at once makes the sweeping conclusion that "this *could not* have occurred, if the administration of baptism to infants had been regarded as a divine institution." In his History he mentions the same persons similarly (p. 32, 33), to which he might have added the name of the great Augustine, who it seems also was not baptized till he grew up, and his mother was pious. Still such a conclusion is quite wrong, though the number of such cases had been more numerous than they were. Christian and pious parents in their circumstances might and did neglect their duty in relation to the baptism of their children, not from the belief that it was not a divine institution for infants, but from other controlling influences. I will illustrate this by a parallel case in connection with the other sacrament of the Lord's Supper, with which, brethren, some of you and probably many of you are yourselves well acquainted. Among the Highlanders of Scotland, for example, (and I believe of their representatives in many parts of Canada), it has been for many generations the practice of a considerable proportion of the truly pious among them to refrain from becoming communicants of the Lord's Table. On this, 1 can bear personal testimony. Yet their ministers have been in the habit of constantly calling on them, and on all that love Jesus to come forward in appropriate spirit, and obey his dying and binding command, "Do this in remembrance of me." Still many, of whose true godliness there is no doubt, hold back and do it not. Should we conclude of them, therefore, that this could not occur if they regarded the administration of the Lord's Supper as a divine institution? If we did we would greatly err. The same persons would themselves seriously and sincerely inform you that on that they have not the slightest doubt, and believe it their duty to observe it, too; but that that *duty* implies a certain worthiness of spirit, which in their judgment they fear they don't sufficiently possess, for which, however, they take the blame to themselves. They have acquired as a rule deeply solemn views and awe of the sacredness of that ordinance, and of its value also as a precious means of grace when appropriately approached and followed by a suitable godly walk and conversation; but at the same time dread the sin of partaking unworthily, and the consequences in eating and drinking judgment to themselves; and this keeps many back from it all their lives.

While we cannot but respect such *motives*, yet we consider that those we speak of, who keep back, mistake the nature of the worthiness required for the Lord's table, as also the probable consequences of *their* approach, while they underestimate the duty of actual obedience. However, the fact is as we have described, and widely prevalent in that section of the Christian church in Fatherland, and no doubt is true of many other believers throughout the Christian world. But, suppose it were the sacrament of baptism that was so regarded, similar consequences would, of course, follow. In that case they would be as much afraid of taking on themselves and their children its conceived responsibilities and probable consquences. Now, what I have just explained of many of my kindred and fellow-Christians, in relation to the Lord's Supper, explains precisely the position of many throughout the whole Church in early ages, in relation to both adult and infant-baptism. The idea of great sacredness and mysterious effects, as the instrument of regeneration was attached to it, and along with that the great heinousness and danger of sins committed after. In short, the leaven we have seen working in Tertullian's mind and treatise on the subject had not died out. Erroneous views of its mysterious sacredness and effects, such as disposed him to counsel people of all ages, and some more particularly than others, to defer it as long as possible, similarly disposed other minds more or less. And it is to be remembered that the circumstances of those days were not so highly favoured as ours are in religious advantages. They had not our widespread education, nor printed Bibles in every Christian home, easily purchased, easily read, etc., etc. For some years at the beginning of the fourth century itself, the civil governments were still all heathen, and the Diocletian persecution raged against the Christians, burning up their pen-printed books or scrolls, and putting many to death. And after the Emperor Constantine appeared and embraced Christianity, as well as before, the Church was chiefly and constantly increased for centuries by conversions from the heathen, many of them not real conversions, who carried with them much of their previous great degradation in ignorance and superstition, which even, in the case of many, truly converted, would not be removed for several generations under favourable circumstances, and many errors in a church of such vast extent, and different languages, etc., might be expected to prevail in such circumstances, and did. Even in our own day, with all our advantages of every kind, and access directly to the Scriptures, every one for ourselves, much error prevails on very important things. Corresponding with this explanation, I find in Cramp's History (p. 81), in a quotation he makes from Neander, that that historian explains the reasons, briefly expressed, why many of that period did not baptize their children, and it may be added why many, like Constantine, deferred their own baptism till on their deathbed. He gives them as follows:—" Partly, the same mistaken notions which arose from confounding the thing represented by baptism with the outward rite, and which afterwards led to the over-valuation of infant-baptism, and partly the frivolous tone of thinking, the indifference to all higher concerns, which characterized so many who had only exchanged the Pagan for a Christian outside." He further adds that, "*in theory it* (infant-baptism) *was* ACKNOWLEDGED TO BE NECESSARY"—by those same parties, who, for the one or the other reason, had neglected to observe it. In other words, it was regarded by them as of divine institution.

Nevertheless, with those exceptions from such reasons, so deeply and clearly impressed was the duty of infant-baptism on the mind of the Church at large, as the doctrine of Scripture and practice of the apostles, that, as we have seen, it continued from the beginning to be everywhere observed, was explained and enforced from the Scriptures and apostles by the great leaders, and other teachers of the Church without a dissentient voice—not even Tertullian's in that connection, and not "any, even the most impious heretics," were heard to deny its divine appointment and validity.

As to those four eminent men, of pious parents, which Cramp specifies as not baptized till manhood, to which I have added the name of Augustine, the weight of their names should really go on the side of infant-baptism if, when they came to think for themselves, and became eminent, they were advocates of it. And that was the fact. Their not being baptized in infancy, and that under the action of "pious" parents, would naturally bias their minds as they grew up to that side of the question, if infant-baptism were regarded by their parents as not divinely appointed, or even as only doubtful. Consequently their becoming strong and powerful advocates of it when they had examined the question for themselves, is all the stronger proof that their advocacy was founded on evidence very thoroughly convincing to them. If, however, their parents' reason for not having had them baptized in infancy was, as no doubt it was, their fear (from an unscriptural superstitious view of the awfulness and peculiar danger of sins after baptism), lest they or their children, through temptation and frailty, should bring on them the divine displeasure and judgment, not for the baptism, but for unfaithfulness to its obligations—that was quite another thing; though their children brought up by them in such ideas would at first be biased accordingly, and would require also all the clearer evidence afterwards to make them infant-baptists, in opposition to such fears.

Now as to the position of those great Christian teachers, I have already placed before you quotations from Chrysostom and Augustine (p. 68-72), two of those referred to,—than which no testimony could be stronger in support of infant baptism. But of Gregory, of Nazianzen, Cramp remarks (Hist. p. 32), "He expressly intimated his disapproval of infant baptism, in one of his public discourses, and advised that children should not be baptized till they were THREE years old or more, at which time they might be able to answer the questions proposed to candidates." In reference to this he refers his readers to "Ullmann's *Gregory of Nazianzen*," p. 27; but does not himself quote any from Ullmann that his readers might judge for themselves what he did teach; which is an important consideration in Cramp's case, as we have had occasion to see before. But looking at the statement he gives in his own words, not Ullmann's, it surely is opposed to Baptist doctrine. It would seem from it that Gregory favoured baptism at "*three* years of age." Well, for certain that does not accord either with Baptist doctrine or practice. When do we ever see or hear or read of Baptists baptizing at such an early age? But Cramp has here adopted the policy I have had to complain so often before of him and others, viz., of concealing by withholding the evidence, and distorting what he gives. I will now add a little also about Gregory *from Cramp's own authority*, *Ullmann*, to see for ourselves what he really says. It is as follows:—" Gregory of Nazianzen (Oratio LX.), OPPOSED THE DELAY OF BAPTISM, which (delay) was founded partly on deference paid to the sacrament, partly on incorrect views and immoral tendencies, partly on absurd prejudices. (Compare Ullmann, p. 466, ss.). Concerning the baptism of infants, Gregory declared 'that it was better that they should be sanctified *without their own consciousness*, than that they should depart being neither sealed nor consecrated (Ullmann. p. 713). In support of his view he appealed to the rite of circumcision which was performed on the eighth day, etc. Gregory nevertheless thought that healthy children *might* wait till the third year, or somewhere thereabout, because they would be able then to *hear* and to *utter something* of the *words used at the performance of the rite*, though they *might not* perfectly *understand* them, but get rather *a general impression* of them." (*Hagenbach's Hist. of Doct.* Vol. I. p. 364). Where now is there room for Cramp's assertion that "Gregory EXPRESSLY intimated his disapproval of infant Baptism!—in support of which he appealed to circumcision on the *eighth day*, and opposed its delay. And in the special case of healthy children who might be allowed to wait till *three* years old, does he say, it was that " they might be able to *answer* the *questions proposed to Candidates,*" which of course would imply an *understanding* of those questions and what answers to make, AT THREE YEARS OF AGE! *There is nothing of that;* but "that they might be able then to HEAR and UTTER *something* of the words used* at the administration though *not understanding their import then,* but to get, it might be, some general impression of them on their feeble minds, those words being few, as, "I baptize thee in the name of the Father," etc. But once more, Dr. Schaff (Hist. of the Chr. Church, Vol. II., p. 483), states as follows: " Many Christian parents postponed the baptism of their children, sometimes from indifference, sometimes from fear that they might by their later life forfeit the grace of baptism and thereby make their condition the worse. Thus Gregory, Nazianzen and Augustine, though they had eminently pious mothers, were not baptized till their conversion in their manhood. But they afterward regretted this. Gregory admonishes a mother: ' Let not sin gain the mastery in thy child; let him be consecrated even in SWADDLING BANDS. Thou art afraid of the divine SEAL on account of the weakness of nature. What weakness of faith! Hannah dedicated her Samuel to the Lord even before his birth ; and immediately after his birth trained him for the priesthood. Instead of fearing human weakness trust in God.'"

So it seems that Gregory was an Infant baptist, and Cramp very unreliable.

Of the other two, Basil of Cæsarea and Ephrem of Edesse, Cramp does not say that they opposed infant baptism, which he would, no doubt, if plausibly possible.

I have now, brethren, come to the close of the work I had undertaken. In the latter section of it I have endeavoured to meet the oft repeated assertion consequently believed in by the body of the Baptist people, from hearing it so affirmed in confident manner by their teachers,—that " Infant Baptism is of PAPAL ORIGIN." I may say that these words are the burden of a communication from a Baptist doctor of divinity, in its issue of the 17th of February last, (now before me) of the *Canadian Baptist*, of Toronto, to which the editor states he gives a place with much pleasure." And this is the leading religious weekly of the Baptist denomination in this Province. The expression of "papal origin," every one will understand to mean, having its origin or beginning in the popish church of Rome, whose popes have claimed to be supreme bishops and head of all the church of Christ. But I have shewn you that such claim was not put forward till after A.D. 597, (when Gregory, bishop of Rome, declared that "whosoever claimed to be universal bishop was the forerunner of antichrist,) that is till the beginning of the *seventh* century. The date universally agreed upon by all Protestant historians, for that position is A.D. 606, under pope Boniface III. Now it was not till A.D. 311, or the beginning of the fourth century, that the hitherto pagan Roman empire declared first in favour of Christianity, under Constantine the Great. Before then the Christian church throughout all lands was continually subject to persecutions, especially at Rome, the seat of the imperial government, which was pagan. There was no Papal Rome then, but pagan Rome. But long before that period we have seen the Councils of Carthage, Cyprian and his sixty-two brother bishops, with *Fidus* bearing testimony, in A.D. 253, to the universal prevalence of infant baptism then, that is to say about sixty years before the Imperial government of the civilized world had declared for Christianity. Again, Origen, taking the Baptist Pengilly's date for his writings on baptism, to be A.D. 230, gave his testimony to its universal prevalence in his day from the apostles' time, and was baptised himself the same year he was born, A.D. 185,—or eighty-five years after the apostolic age. Tertulian again wrote earlier still, A.D. 200, or 111 years before Rome had given up its heathen idols in the Pantheon, and bore decided testimony also to its prevalence then,—400 years before Papal Rome had raised its head. Then before that again in A.D. 177, 140, we have seen the testimony of Irenæus and Justin Martyr of their day, extending into the apostolic age. How then can that be said to be of Papal origin which existed, and existed too so long before the papal church of Rome itself? Then there is the testimony of the close of the fourth century, Augustine, Chrysostom, Pelagius, etc., etc., also so full and conclusive. Besides most of these various witnesses did not belong to the jurisdiction of the church in Rome at all. They were bishops and claimed equality with that in Rome. Justin Martyr was resident in Rome, but *very long* before it was papal. Irenæus was of Lyons, in France; Tertullian and Cyprian were of Carthage, in North Africa. Origen was most of his public lifetime in Alexandria, near Palestine. Chrysostom was bishop of Constantinople, as was his predecessor Gregory Nazianzen. Augustine was bishop of Hippo, within 200 miles from Carthage. None of these nor of the churches elsewhere, recognized Rome's jurisdiction as over them; nor did Rome claim it in their days.

I have said enough, I think, brethren, to show you the gross untruthfulness of the frequently repeated assertion that "infant-baptism is of Papal origin—a relic of Popery —of the Church of Rome. It is of a piece with all the rest I have exhibited to you of great and deliberate misrepresentation like that of Cramp, Pengilly, etc., in this Anabaptist cause; and I have material at hand by which I could show you ten times more than I have now exhibited, only the expense and the want of time hinder further enlargement. The cause that inspires its advocates, its leading men, its church publication societies, its ministers, etc., to adopt such methods of advancement is not good—is not from above, but from beneath, whence such inspiration, such a spirit comes. It recalls to mind the profession on the one hand, and the spirit and plans of action on the other, of those of old, of whom the Saviour said, they compassed sea and land to make proselytes, but who, when made, were worse than before; yes, and reminds strongly of the spirit and tactics of Rome herself— her "pious frauds" and unholy tactics. The motto seems in each case alike, 'The end sanctifies the means.' If numerical success is gained, that seems to be everything with the prime movers, while the many sins committed as the means of obtaining it are not regretted, but accounted serviceable, and zealously persevered in without flinching or deviation.

And yet it must be added that the great body of the Baptist people are quite ignorant of the deceptions practised on them. They are not in circumstances to ascertain the truth for themselves. Though they had the time, the education, and willingness to take the trouble, they have not the original works within their reach to inquire into for themselves, and are too willing, alas! to believe with readiness what seems to favour the side they have espoused. While the representations continually made to them in books and other publications, and by word of mouth from their zealous teachers, are so presented to them—the truth suppressed—the facts distorted—that I don't wonder that even good men and women are misled and rendered zealous even to fanaticism on the side of wrong. And I have no doubt very many even of their ministers are equally deceived; who form their opinions—for they are but men—from the representations of a few leaders. To ascertain the real facts involves to ministers the expense of getting the various necessary sources of original information, the considerable trouble and time necessary for inquiry into them, which, with other constantly pressing duties, is not easily secured, and withal requires a mind devotedly attached to truth, and deeply sensitive to the greatness of the sin of "bearing false witness against our neighbour." The temptation to take second, third, or fourth hand information, and save all this inconvenience, and, at the same time, to make proselytes the more readily thereby, is considerable, and too often prevails. Yes, and prevails, too, even with the leaders, as with Dr. Taylor, for example, in his "Baptists: Who they are, and what they have done;" who, at great length, implicitly reproduces Dr. Cramp, with his misrepresentations, and here and there on important points adds decidedly to the misrepresentations, by going farther in that way than Dr. Cramp, his professed authority, has done, and even contrary to his admissions; for instance, as specimens, he affirms on Cramp's authority (p. 31) that the Novatians and Donatists WERE Baptists, though Cramp (Hist., p. 45, 46) reluctantly admits there is no proof of this; and history shows abundant proof of the opposite. Or, as seen in Cramp and Pengilly's use of Booth's "Paedobaptist Examined;" which is also very unfair in its quotations. They give many quotations from that work on Booth's authority, without improving his errors, while they are silent on him where he would contradict the assertions they make; as, for instance, the case I set before you of Deylingius on baptism, by sprinkling, in the Greek church. Booth, again, may have quoted much from others, second-hand, and so the ball of misrepresentation rolls on, gathering as it progresses, till it reaches the confiding common people, who take what is presented to them as, no doubt, reliable and fairly exhibited.

CONCLUSION OF LECTURE.

Part III.

EXTENSION OF THE SUBJECT. ADDITIONAL PROOFS.

We can anticipate the Baptists reply after all we have shown on Infant Baptism, that uninspired history is not a proof of Scriptural authority. Let your appeal be to the Scriptures alone. This sounds well to the ear and implies what they affirm, that the Word of God is not in favour of Infant baptism. Our object in the preceding Lecture has been to demonstrate that its origin was NOT PAPAL, and also how leading Baptist writers deal with that subject in books sanctioned and issued widely by their church's Publication Societies. It is hardly honourable in them to make and repeat the charge a thousand times, that infant baptism is a relic of the Popish church of Rome, and then when we have proven its universal observance all over Christendom several centuries before the church in Rome became papal, to say, "O though you have established its existence and prevalence long before that period, that does not decide its Scriptural authority." But what about that calumny of its origin? We cannot be expected to find the history of the second, third, and succeeding centuries in the Bible, which was completed at the end of the first century, but we have found abundant proof in even Baptist books with all their disposition to suppress and distort, that that charge is a calumny of much guilt, and one I have no doubt that will continue to be perpetuated for long.

But it is said, Give an express precept or example of infant baptism in the Scriptures clear and specific, and that if that cannot be given then there is no Scripture warrant for it; that uninspired history proves nothing in establishing its Scripturality. That is to say, no religious observance has Scripture authority on which we have not in Scripture express precept enjoining it, or inspired example. Well, let us examine this argument in regard, for instance, to

THE FIRST DAY OF THE WEEK AS THE SABBATH DAY;

under the obligations of the fourth commandment of the Moral Law. This is a very important question, still more so considerably than the baptism of water, without underestimating the latter. For centuries there has been and still is a denomination called the Seventh day Baptists, who hold that day and not the first to be the Scriptural Christian Sabbath. But the other Baptist denominations like ourselves and other Christians regard it as the first day of the week. On this I might quote you from two Baptist Confessions of Faith before me, but it is unnecessary; it is well known. They refer to the terms of the fourth commandment, as obligatory on it (Exod. xx. 8), as ours also does; namely:—"Remember the Sabbath day to keep it holy; . . . in it thou shalt not do any work," etc. You know that commandment was first applicable to the seventh day and continued so throughout all the Old Testament. The authority for the change of the day must therefore be sought in the New Testament. I will exhibit to you all it says on the subject. And, first, as seemingly in the words (but not really) against that change the seventh day is often called "the sabbath day," after our Lord's death and ascension, while in all the Scriptures the first day of the week is not once called by that name, nor is the fourth commandment *expressly* ever applied to it. The Jews who were not Christians still observed as before the seventh day as the Sabbath, and the apostles and their brethren joined their meetings for worship and to preach to them Jesus as opportunity was afforded. On which, for instance, as follows (Acts xiii. 13, 14): "But when Paul and his company departed from Perga, they came to Antioch in Pisidia, and went into the *synagogue* on *the sabbath day*, and sat down." In his address to them Paul said (ver. 27), "For they that dwell at Jerusalem, and their rulers, because they knew him (Jesus) not, nor yet the voices of the prophets which are read every sabbath day, they have fulfilled them in condemning him." "And (ver. 42, 44) when the Jews were gone out of the synagogue, the Gentiles besought that these words might be preached to them the next sabbath." "And the next sabbath day came almost the whole city together to hear the word of God." Now in each of these passages the reference is to the Jewish Sabbath; yet the inspired historian and speaker call it "the sabbath day" without any qualification, and through the Acts (chaps. xv. 21; xvii. 2; xviii. 4; etc.), we see the same mode of speech. The Apostles and Christians in Judea and all countries where Jews were settled, still honoured the seventh day Sabbath, and we read of no complaint against them for not doing so, on which the Jews were very jealous. They also honoured the temple in Jerusalem by attending it, (Acts ii. 46; iii. 1), and observed several things of the Mosaic economy. Thus when Paul had just returned from the heathen, James and the elders said to him (Acts xxi. 20), "Thou seest, brother, how many thousands of Jews there are *which believe*; and they are all zealous of the law: and they are informed of thee that thou teachest all the Jews which are among the Gentiles to forsake Moses, saying that they ought not to circumcise their children, neither to walk after the customs. What is it therefore? the multitude must needs come together: for they will hear that thou art come. Do therefore this that we say to thee: We have four men which have a vow on them: them take, and purify thyself with them that they may shave their heads; and all may know that those things, whereof they were informed concerning thee, are nothing; but that thou thyself also walkest orderly and keepest the law. As touching the *Gentiles* which believe, we have written and concluded that *they* observe *no such thing*, save only that they keep themselves from things offered to idols, and from blood, and from strangled, and from fornication. And Paul took the men, and the next day, purifying himself with them, entered into the temple, to signify the accomplishment of the days of purification, until that an offering should be offered for every one of them." It appears that Paul also had a vow, and had to keep the feast at that time at Jerusalem (xviii. 18, 21). Of this conduct of the inspired guides of the Church, we know the reason. Circumcision was permitted to the children of Jewish Christians on account of the deep hold its original divine appointment and long observance had on their mind and conscience. And so of other things. The seventh day Sabbath was in these respects in the same position. It was very specifically and strictly enjoined in the Fourth Commandment, and had been the day observed as such from the time of Moses, and from the creation. It was, of course, quite lawful for Christians to worship and preach the Gospel on that day under the New Testament dispensation, or on any day. The apostles refused to perpetuate or permit the observances peculiar to the Mosaic economy among the Gentile Christians, but, by the wise and gracious will of Christ, bore with the infirmities of the Jewish believers' mind till they should grow out of them by time, and increase of grace, and knowledge of the truth, as it is in Jesus. Also, the Fourth Commandment on the seventh day was the law of the land of Judea, enforced by government, so that no one was permitted to work secularly. The apostles, then, still honoured it, as we have seen, and they still called it "the sabbath day."

Let me now, on the other hand, place before you all the Scriptures (they are not many) bearing on the first day of the week, as the day substituted for the seventh. I will put them all together, that they may be seen in one view. Of the day our Saviour rose from the dead we read, "Then, the same day at evening, *being* the first day of the week, when the doors were shut where the disciples were assembled for fear of the Jews, came Jesus and stood in the midst, and said, Peace be unto you," etc. "And *after eight* days, again, His disciples were within, and Thomas with them; then came Jesus, the doors being shut, and stood in the midst," etc. (John xx. 19, 26). The next reference is in the Acts (xx. 6, 7), "And we sailed away from Philippi after the days of unleavened bread, and came unto them to Troas in five days, where we abode *seven* days. And upon the first day of the week, when the disciples came together to break bread, Paul preached unto them, ready to depart on the morrow; and continued his speech till midnight." Then, after he had restored Eutychus to life, who had fallen down from the third loft, on that occasion, it is continued (ver. 11), "When he, Paul, therefore, was come up again, and had broken bread and eaten, and talked a long while, even till break of day, so he departed." He was on his way to Jerusalem. The next is in 1 Cor. xvi. 1, 2, "Now, concerning the collection for the saints, as I have given order to the churches of Galatia, even so do ye. Upon the first day of the week let every one of you lay by him in store as God hath prospered him, that there be no gatherings when I come." These are all the passages in which the first day of the week is *specified*. The last passage on the subject is John's testimony (Rev. i. 10.), "I was in the Spirit on *the Lord's day*, and heard behind me a great voice, as of a trumpet."

Now, let it be borne in mind that what Baptists require in regard to the baptism of infants is that to warrant it there must be a precept enjoining it in regard to them in *express terms;* or an inspired example, in which infants are expressly stated to have been baptized. They do not agree to proof by inference or implication. Well, in the last passage, or elsewhere, the day of the week John calls "*the Lord's day*," is not specified, nor is this name found in any other place in the New Testament. In the Fourth Commandment in the Old Testament we read, "the seventh day is the sabbath of the Lord thy God;" which also meant *the Lord's day*. There is, therefore, no proof in Scripture that the *first* day is the Lord's day, IF nothing will be taken as proof but an express declaration. Yet (by the way) Baptists, like ourselves, call it by this name, and say there is Scriptural authority for it. In this they are right, but it is neither from express precept nor example, but but by a kind of proof quite different from their requirement for infant-baptism, which I will show you in a little. The passage in 1 Cor. xvi. 2, "Let every one of you lay by him in store as God hath prospered him"—for the assistance of the poor saints at Jerusalem,—does not *specify* whether this was to be done privately, or by publicly giving their contributions on that day to the office-bearers of the Church, to be kept in store by them; nor where or how the "gatherings" were to be made. There is no *mention* in the words of meetings for public worship, or abstinence from secular employments. The other passage in the

Acts does not say the disciples came together on that day to break bread, *because* it was the Sabbath, or because it was the first day of the week, (though I have no doubt it was,) but simply that on that day they assembled for that purpose. It is not unscriptural, however, to partake of the Lord's supper on other days than the Sabbath. Our Lord at first dispensed it on a Thursday,—" the night in which he was betrayed;" and while the Sabbath, being usually the most appropriate, is usually chosen for it, it has often been most lawfully partaken of on other days— as in times of persecution and other special circumstances. It might be said, not without reason, that Paul's short visit to Troas and his departure " on the morrow," when the disciples there " would see his face no more " (ch. xx. 25, 38), was a great occasion most suitably preceded by their thus together showing forth their Redeemer's death and love the last day before the Apostle and his accompanying brethren left. On the other hand, however, the fact that they " abode seven days " there, or an exact week, and that this day was chosen for that special ordinance, does seem to direct our attention to the day itself as especially important, and makes it appear probable that Paul had deferred his departure till the next day from regard to the first day as set apart for sacred purposes; rather than that they met together on that occasion simply because it happened to be the one before Paul had resolved to sail. The reference in 1 Corinthians, drawing special attention to that day, again adds weight to this view. But observe, this is all *inference*. It is not expressly stated. The 'seventh day' Baptists must have direct and express declaration. Moreover, the disciples seem to have met together in the after part of that day, as Paul preached till midnight and spoke till the " break of the day following;" and there is no proof that they were not engaged in secular labour in the early part of the day or were not to do so. It is contended that there is no explicit statement such as—" 'Remember the first day of the week to keep it holy, as the Sabbath of the Lord, instead of the seventh; in it thou shalt not do any work,' etc.—while there is such a command in the Scriptures as to the seventh day." Again, while it does not seem singular that the Saviour should come to his disciples on the day he arose from the dead, there is something striking in the manner of expression, viz.: "The same day at evening, *being the first day of the week* .... came Jesus and stood in their midst." Attention seems thus drawn to this day as a particular reason of his so coming then. Weight is added to this again, when we read that he reserved his second appearance among them for the eighth day after, or the first day of the week following. Yet there is nothing said of the Sabbath and its obligations. Also, he afterwards appeared to and communed with them (John xxi.) on a different day of the week, so far as appears, when they were fishing on the sea of Tiberias.

To sum up. On the one hand, the apostles and the inspired writer of the Acts when referring to the seventh day always called it still "the Sabbath day." This, however, does not decide that it was now really the Sabbath of the New Dispensation. Christians, for example, have ever been accustomed to call the days of the week by the name originally given them by the heathen in honour of their gods—Monday, Tuesday, Wednesday, Thursday,—after the gods Thor, Weden, the Moon, etc.—without our meaning by this that these days should be kept sacred to those gods, but merely to distinguish the days as generally called and known by these names. In Judea, and wherever Jews resided, there was a similar reason for calling the seventh day the Sabbath, and all the more that it had been hitherto ever the Sabbath appointed by the living and true God,—of the Christians as well as the Jews. Still the question remains, Was that *the* reason? The Apostles and Christians generally honoured that day in public worship, and preaching in the synagogue, etc. Further, there is no express declaration that the Sabbath was changed from the seventh to the first day. These are the facts on the one side. On the other hand, the first day of the week appears to have had a particular prominence of a religious nature and observance. We never find the second, third, fourth, fifth or sixth day pointed out specifically in this way. Moreover, the day of Pentecost, when the Holy Spirit was poured out in New Testament fulness, was the first day of the week, (Lev. xxiii. 15, 16,) as well as that chosen by our Lord for his first and second appearance in the midst of his assembled disciples after his resurrection. Yet, withal, as far as Scripture statements of every kind go, we can only INFER the change of *the Sabbath* to that day. IT IS NOT EXPRESSLY STATED TO BE CHANGED. If we had no other kind of evidence, with the fourth commandment before us in its explicitness on the seventh day, and all the old Testament reaffirming it with such solemn emphasis, and the apostles, etc., calling it the Sabbath day and practically honouring it seemingly as such, we would be at a loss to know for certain (whatever we might think about the first) that the seventh was no longer intended to be observed as such. Yet, like ourselves, Baptists generally maintain that it is so changed, and practise accordingly; labouring in worldly employments on the Saturday, refraining from them on the first day of the week, and keeping it 'holy' for and in the worship of God. But how may the question be further

CLEARED UP OTHERWISE ?

It is by this—*The Early History of the Church*. If we find satisfactory evidence immediately after the apostles, just as they have left the spheres of their superintendence, that Christians all over the world—in Palestine, Asia, Rome, Africa, etc., all habitually assembled together for worship on the first day of the week, and kept it sacred in terms of the Fourth Commandment, we have irresistible proof that that doctrine and practice were from apostolic authority and example. For it cannot reasonably be supposed that so important an institution as the Christian Sabbath could, in so short a time after the apostles left, have come into universal observance instead of the Jewish Sabbath, without the sanction of the apostles, considering, too, the strictness of the divine command on the Sabbath. This our Baptist friends admit equally with ourselves. And on the

SUFFICIENCY OF THE HISTORICAL EVIDENCE ON THIS,

let me quote you from the BAPTIST writer, J. Torrey Smith, on the inside cover of Pengilly's " Scripture Guide to Baptism." He says, " Those Christian writings of the first century after the apostles (though few in number) clearly show that the Lord's day, or Christian Sabbath, was from the first observed."

Let me give you some specimens of this evidence, which is outside of Scripture, but undoubted. Pliny, a heathen governor of Bithynia, (a province of Asia,) and a persecutor, having been directed by the emperor Trajan judicially to investigate the conduct of the Christians, did so. His epistle in reply we have, of date A.D. 107, or only seven years after the decease of the apostle John. Where he describes the Christians' worship, he says, " they were accustomed to meet together on a stated day at sunrise, sang a song to Christ as God," etc. " Afterwards, at evening, they assembled again." This shows they set apart that whole day for divine worship. Again, the great Ignatius, bishop of Antioch, was put to death by Trajan, being thrown to wild beasts. The precise year of his martyrdom is uncertain, but was some time before A.D. 117, when Trajan died. He was himself a disciple and a companion of the apostles. Speaking of the seventh day Sabbath, he said, " The Christians celebrate no longer the Sabbath, but the Lord's day, on which their life arose to them by him." That is, instead of the Jewish Sabbath they observed the Lord's day, regarding under that name *the day He rose* from the dead. We have here, therefore, evidence on the day referred to by John as *the Lord's*, in Rev. i. 10.; and this testimony was written only a few years after John wrote that book, and indicates that this was the name commonly applied to *it* throughout the Church. Justin Martyr, we have seen before, wrote his " Apology" to the Roman emperor and people in A.D. 140, or only forty years after the death of John, while he was born himself, at most, three or four years after. The Roman names for the first and second days of the week were Sunday, Moonday, from whom we have derived them and the others in our use. On the subject before us, Justin states in his " Apology" as follows :—" On the day which is called Sunday, ALL, whether dwelling in the towns or in the villages, hold meetings; and the memoirs of the apostles and the writings of the prophets are read, as long as the time permits," etc. " We assemble in common on Sunday, because this is the first day in which God created the world, and the light, and because Jesus Christ our Saviour, on the same day, rose from the dead and appeared to His disciples." After describing the different devotional exercises engaged in, he also says:—"The wealthy and the willing then give contributions according to their free will, and the collection is deposited with the president, who, therewith, supplies orphans and widows, poor and needy, prisoners and strangers, and takes care of all who are in want." Let these specimens suffice. The Church at this time was established in many lands, north, south, east and west, when it had just emerged as a mighty ocean stream from under the eyes and inspired personal instruction and guidance of the apostles, who had been over it everywhere for many years, as the Acts and Epistles indicate; and at the beginning of that period we see all, with one consent, in these terms holding sacred the first day of the week. The Jewish Christians we find, indeed, observing in different places the seventh day during the second century, etc., and letting it go with reluctance, but, like all the others, they kept the first day sacred as well. They had no difficulty about the first day, but were attached to the seventh for the reasons I have before explained, which gradually gave way.

Now, this broad comprehensive fact being admitted, we can, with it before us, go back to those passages in the New Testament on the first day of the week, and can legitimately regard them as containing *more* than they *literally* express—a common thing in Scripture. The expression, "the Lord's day," by John, we see, as already remarked, was meant of this day, though he does not specify it himself. The practice of Christians, explained by Justin Martyr, to bring their contributions for the assistance of the needy to the Church on this day, and "lay by them in store,"—deposit them in the hands of the presiding pastor, fits in with Paul's direction in 1 Cor. xvi. 2, and is a reliable light-giving commentary on it. In like manner on Acts xx. 7, "And upon the first day of the week, when the disciples came together to break bread, Paul preached to them till midnight," etc. When we see the universal observance of the first day as the Sabbath at the end of the same century, we have no difficulty in perceiving its observance as such by the disciples indicated there.

As to the passages in John xx. and xxi., although the Lord's third appearance to His disciples was not on the first day of the week; the first two were, and were well fitted, as they were, no doubt, intended, to prepare the minds of His disciples and the Church for the change of day as Sabbath, and to give strength to the proof of it afterwards and otherwise brought out in the manner we describe. When we see it established that the first day of the week is indeed made the Sabbath, we also see a particular meaning pointing in that direction, in our Lord, after appearing to His assembled disciples the day he arose, reserving His next appearance for the next first day of the week. And then, when we consider the nature of the event that occurred in His resurrection, we see the suitableness of the change. If it was proper that the seventh day should be set apart before and hallowed in memorial of God's finished work of creation, how much more should He appoint a similar sacred memorial for His homage praise and grace in the day He rested from His still greater work of redemption; by which is secured glory to God in the highest, and on earth peace, good-will towards men? In these two works of God there is a parallelism, only that the last excels the first in glory, and hence appropriately the memorials are similar in nature, one day in seven set apart for divine worship, and the first day of the week, as commemorating the completion of the more glorious work, henceforward became more appropriately the Sabbath than the seventh day, while it includes the objects of the seventh in regard to God as Creator, as well as Redeemer—or *all* His glory and goodness. However, while we can see the suitableness of that day from the nature of the case, we must look elsewhere for the proof of its having been so set apart; which is found cumulatively, to a certain extent, in the references we find to that day in Scripture, which are made decisive by the universal observance of it as the Sabbath of the New Testament dispensation at the end of the first century, *which it is admitted* necessarily implied the inspired sanction and authority of the apostles for the same. Looking at the Saviour's death, which took place on Friday—the sixth day—when He said on the cross, "It is finished," we might also see suitable reason for the appointment of that day as Sabbath in commemoration, but that would be no proof of its appointment. We would require to have proof otherwise of this being done, which we have not. We might reason similarly of the day of His birth, which was certainly a very great event, as the angel declared to the shepherds, and the other angels sang. But no reference to a commemorative Christmas appears *at all* in His Word, while the first reference to Christmas does not appear in the Church till the fourth century.

We have thus seen, brethren, the value of the evidence we have on the Christian Sabbath at the beginning of the second century—its usefulness in helping us to see the force of those passages in Scripture on this subject, and how we have not in Scripture an express precept specifying that the Fourth Commandment is transferred from the seventh to the first day, neither have we an express inspired example, covering that ground beyond question. Now,

LET US APPLY ALL THIS IN REGARD TO INFANT-BAPTISM.

There is no express precept in Scripture, "Baptize the infants of believers;" and no example where it is *expressly* specified that an infant was among those baptized. Our Baptist friends, therefore, conclude that such ought not to be baptized. Well, there is no express precept, "The first day of the week thou shalt keep holy as the Sabbath of the Lord thy God, instead of the seventh day hitherto commanded; in it thou shalt not do any work," etc. Nor, is there any example where it is expressly specified that the first day was so substituted and observed in those terms. Shall we, therefore, conclude that the first day of the week ought not to be kept as the Sabbath, but that the seventh should? Our Baptist friends, at least, will surely answer Yes; as, if this kind of argument be conclusive in the former case, which they strongly and continually affirm it is, it will surely be regarded by them as equally conclusive in regard to any other institution and observance. We should expect, therefore, they will not reject infant-baptism on account of its importance, as without Scripture authority, on the ground that there is no express precept or express example specifying its administration, and at the same time, not teach and act similarly about the sacred Sabbath day, as being a less important religious institution. For in that there would be two great errors, both plain to be seen, namely, first, the Sabbath is not only not less, but still more important than baptism, without depreciating the latter; and, second, the nature of any kind of argument as a sound or unsound one, as right or wrong, is, of course, never to be estimated according to the supposed importance or unimportance of the matters reasoned upon. But what do we really find as to the Sabbath? Our Baptist friends, with but a small exception, reply, No; not the seventh, but the first day of the week must be kept in terms of the Fourth Commandment, as of inspired authority; and, in the absence of *express* statements in Scripture sufficient to establish this, they, like ourselves, appeal to the evidence in

THE WRITINGS OF THE SECOND AND SUBSEQUENT CENTURIES

of its observance on that day by the Church throughout, from immediately after the apostolic age, WHICH they, like ourselves affirm brings out to view a fulness of meaning in connection with what is stated in Scripture, which is not conveyed by itself expressly. That is, they object to, as an argument for infant-baptism, what themselves willingly use as a genuine and decisive argument for the Christian Sabbath! Moreover, as a matter of fact, the whole SCRIPTURE evidence for infant-baptism is MUCH MORE ABUNDANT THAN THAT ON THE CHRISTIAN SABBATH. And as to the examples of baptism recorded there, while the terms employed in several instances admit the idea of infants in their natural and usual signification, in no case do we find an exception made of infants, by refusal to baptize them, or one specified as left unbaptized, where its parent and other members of his or her household were baptized together. Into this line of evidence we will now look a little. And first let us take

THE CASE OF LYDIA AND HER HOUSEHOLD,

(Acts xvi. 14, 15), "And a certain woman named Lydia, a seller of purple, of the city of Thyatira, which worshipped God, heard us, whose heart the Lord opened, that she attended unto the things which were spoken of Paul. And when she was baptized and her household, she besought us saying, If ye have judged me to be faithful to the Lord, come into my house, and abide there." Now, it is undoubted that the term "household" is quite applicable to a family of the youngest children. Therefore, so far as this term indicates, Lydia may have had infant children, and if she had, they were evidently baptized with herself. So this passage, if it does not expressly indicate infant-baptism in precise terms, does not discountenance it certainly, but rather favours it, as the term "household" admits freely the idea of children of any age. Again, it is particularly specified that *she* worshipped God, that *she* heard Paul, that the Lord opened *her* heart, that *she* attended to the things spoken by Paul; and then that she was baptized and her household. On the other hand, the only thing affirmed of her household in all this is that they were baptized with her, there being no mention of any faith or other thing but her own. This example, then, does not disfavour the baptism of children on account of their parents' faith, but seems to indicate that Lydia's were baptized with her on account of her having just before become a believer, which would also be consistent with the baptism of such of them as might be very young in age.

Now, no other example of Scripture is found to contradict the apparent teaching of this one. Even suppose it clearly appeared in others, when the parent and household were baptized together, that they had faith, too, which certainly might be, that would not be a contradiction. Their parent's faith could be a sufficient reason for their baptism, as in Lydia's case, and their own faith another sufficient reason in addition. But this would be a contradiction, if an example occurred where it is shown that, while some of the household were baptized with their parent, an infant or infants belonging to it were not. But nowhere does this at all appear.

But along with the evidence in the case of Lydia and her household, not to mention other examples, there is much from other Scriptural sources. There is, for instance,

A STRIKING RESEMBLANCE BETWEEN CIRCUMCISION AND BAPTISM

in their symbolic nature and uses. Both were to be administered but once to the same person. The one was the token of admission into the visible church of the Old Testament (which was the church of Jesus the Messiah), so that he who was not circumcised could not legitimately be allowed its other privileges of membership (Gen. xvii. 10, 11, 14; Rom. iii. 12). Baptism has the same place and force under the New Testament. Again, circumcision, as an emblem, was divinely appointed to represent man's natural sinfulness of heart and life, and that God required in his service, and imparted by his grace to them that sought him, a clean heart and right spirit (Rom. ii. 29); in which they put off the body of the sins of the flesh, or abandon a life of impiety (Colos. ii. 11), and devote themselves in the love of God and his righteousness to a new life of holy obedience (Deut x..16; xxx. 6; Philip. iii. 3). And baptism is appointed to impress these same truths on our minds. To state it in the Baptist Pengilly's words (" Scripture Guide to Baptism," p. 80): " On the spiritual design of baptism. It was to teach the *sinfulness of man*, and the necessity of *purification* from sin, in order to eternal life. . . . Baptism was intended to teach and to signify the Christian's entire *abandonment of a life of impiety*, and *his entrance upon a new life* of devotion and dedication to God." (The words *italicised* are so in Pengilly). Also in Colos. (ii. 10–14) they are both spoken of together as of the same spiritual import, as both teaching a new life in Christ of holiness, with forgiveness of sins through faith of the operation of God.

It also appears that the gospel and church of the Old Testament dispensation were the same as those of the New, only, in several things, under a different external administration, by which we are still instructed in divine things, the same as they were, out of the same Old Testament Scriptures. They had the same Messiah to look to and trust in, the same kind of worship in what was moral and spiritual. Abraham's faith, as the means of his justification and not his own righteousness, is explained at length by the apostle (Rom. iv; Gal. iii.) as the same that believers in Christ have, and which is counted for righteousness to them also. Now, as a matter of fact, Abraham was himself not circumcised till after he became a believer and servant of God; but when he was circumcised, his household were circumcised with him, on account of his faith, not their own, and the command was that it be administered to them soon after their birth. In his case it was, among other things, a sign and seal of the righteousness of his faith ; in their case, as they had not faith when circumcised, it was, among other things, a sign and seal from God of the righteousness of their parent's faith, which thus commended it to their pursuit in after years for themselves.

We have now seen the resemblances in use and spiritual import between circumcision and baptism, and here, in Abraham and his household, there appears as to circumcision a similitude of administration to that of baptism in the example of Lydia and her household. And there can be no doubt from the nature of baptism as to what it is meant to signify that it was also a sign and seal (or divine assurance) of the righteousness of Lydia's faith, as of all believers, which is just the same as Abraham had.

Another thing circumcision was pointed to signify, was, said the Lord to Abraham, "And I will establish my covenant between me and thee, and thy seed after thee in their generations for an everlasting covenant, to be a God unto thee and to thy seed after thee." "This is my covenant, which ye shall keep between me and you, and thy seed after thee. Every man child among you shall be circumcised. And ye shall circumcise the flesh of your foreskin ; and *it shall be* A TOKEN OF THE COVENANT *betwixt me and you*." Baptists say that this covenant and its token had reference only to earthly, not to spiritual blessings, although we see the token, circumcision, was a sign and seal of the righteousness of faith, and of the new heart and right spirit God requires, and by his grace imparts. But surely it is a poor idea that GOD would mean only earthly things, without spiritual blessings, by his promise, "I will be A GOD to thee and to thy seed after thee." And how different from his own exhibitions of it all through the Old Testament, and in the New Testament (for instance, in Rom. iv; xi. 26–29; Gal. iii. 29; Heb. xi. 8, 16). In conformity with this promise it was that he afterwards gave to Israel his law, and appointed the various institutions of his worship, means of grace unto salvation (Micah vii. 18–20) ; while the rest of the world remained in the darkness and ruin of idolatry. Hence the apostle says (Rom. iii. 1–4), "What advantage, then, hath the

Jew ? or *what profit* is there OF CIRCUMCISION ? *Much every way*, CHIEFLY *because that* UNTO THEM WERE COMMITTED THE ORACLES OF GOD." This will show of itself that circumcision had reference CHIEFLY to spiritual blessings pertaining to eternal salvation. So you see, brethren, that Baptists, to support their theory against infant-baptism, etc., say much that will not bear the test of examination of Scripture.

To bring out that in that covenant promise to Abraham was meant

THE GOSPEL BLESSINGS OF HEAVEN ABOVE,

as well as the earth beneath, and to show that under the Old Testament dispensation God clearly declared that He would bless *the offspring* of his believing and obedient people, as well as themselves, I will place before you a number of passages from the Old Testament, containing that precious promise. Let the first referred to be that in Genes. xvii., before quoted, to which I add the following:—

"And now, Israel, what doth the Lord thy God require of thee, but to fear the Lord thy God, to walk in all his ways, and to love him, and to serve the Lord thy God with all thy heart and with all thy soul, to keep the commandments of the Lord, and his statutes, which I command thee this day for thy good ? Behold the heaven and the heaven of heavens is the Lord thy God's, the earth also, with all that therein is. Only the Lord had a delight in thy fathers to love them, *and he chose their seed after them*, even you above all people, as it is this day. Circumcise, therefore, the foreskin of your *heart*, and be no more stiffnecked," etc. (Deut. x. 12–16. See also iv. 31, 37). "What man is he that feareth the Lord ? him shall he teach in the way that he shall choose. His soul shall dwell at ease; and his seed shall inherit the earth." " I have been young, and now am old ; yet have I not seen the righteous forsaken, nor his seed begging bread. He is ever merciful, and lendeth ; and his seed is blessed." "God will save Zion, and will build the cities of Judah ; that they may dwell there and have it in possession. The *seed* also of His servants *shall* INHERIT IT (Zion) ; and they that love His name shall dwell therein." "The *children* of thy servants shall continue, and THEIR *seed* shall be established before thee." "But the mercy of the Lord is from everlasting to everlasting upon them that fear Him, and His RIGHTEOUSNESS unto CHILDREN'S *children*." "Blessed is the man that feareth the Lord, that delighteth greatly in his commandments. His seed shall be mighty upon earth: the generation of the upright shall be blessed." (Psalms xxv. 12, 13; xxxvii. 25, 26; lxix. 35, 36; cii. 38; ciii. 17; cxii. 1, 2).

"Though hand join in hand, the wicked shall not be unpunished; but the seed of the righteous shall be delivered." "In the fear of the Lord is strong confidence: and his children shall have a place of refuge." "The just man walketh in his integrity; and his children are blessed after him." (Proverbs xi. 21; xiv. 26; xx. 7). "Yet, now, hear, O Jacob, my servant; and Israel, whom I have chosen: Thus saith the Lord that made thee and formed thee from the womb, which will help thee; Fear not, O Jacob, my servant; and thou, Jesurun, whom I have chosen. For I will pour water on him that is thirsty, and floods upon the dry ground: I will pour MY SPIRIT upon *thy seed*, and *my blessing* upon *thine offspring:* And *they* shall spring up as among the grass, as willows by the watercourses. One shall say, I am the Lord's; and another shall call himself by the name of Jacob; and another shall subscribe with his hand unto the Lord, and surname himself by the name of Israel." "And the Redeemer shall come to Zion, and unto them that turn from transgression in Jacob, saith the Lord. As for me, THIS *is my covenant* with them, saith the Lord; *My spirit* that is upon thee, and *My words* which I have put in thy mouth, shall not depart out of thy mouth, nor out of the mouth of thy seed, nor out of the mouth of thy seed's seed, saith the Lord, from henceforth and forever." "And their seed shall be known among the Gentiles, and their offspring among the people: all that see them shall acknowledge them, that they are the seed which the Lord hath blessed." "They shall not labour in vain, nor bring forth for trouble, for they are *the seed of* the blessed of the Lord, AND *their offspring* WITH THEM." (Isaiah xliv. 1-5; lix. 20, 21; lxi. 9; lxv. 23). "And now, therefore, thus saith the Lord God of Israel, concerning this city, whereof ye say, It shall be delivered into the hand of the king of Babylon by the sword, and by the famine, and by the pestilence; Behold, I will gather them out of all countries, whither I have driven them in mine anger, and in my fury, and in great wrath; and I will bring them again into this place, and I will cause them to dwell safely: and they shall be my people, *and I will be their God:* And I will give them *one heart*, and *one way*, that they *may fear me* forever, for the good of them, and of their children after them: And I will make an everlasting covenant with them, that I will not turn away from them, to do them good; but I will put my fear in their hearts, that they shall not depart from me. Yea, I will rejoice over them to do them good, and I will plant them in this land assuredly, with my whole heart, and with my whole soul," etc. (Jerem. xxxii. 36-41.) We have in this passage a commentary of God's own, on what He means by the words, "I will be a God unto thee, and to thy seed after thee"—to which He alludes here, in ver. 38).

These are specimens, brethren, of God's gracious, precious statements on this subject in the Old Testament. Some of them, you observe, as those quoted from Genesis, Deuteronomy, and Jeremiah, refer directly to the posterity of Abraham, Isaac, and Jacob; the others, from the Psalms, and Proverbs, and Isaiah, speak similarly of the seed of them that fear the Lord now as well as then; while those in the 59th, 61st, and 65th chapters of Isaiah make particular reference to the continuance of the same divine favours under the New Testament, after Jesus the Messiah would have come; which will be seen still more fully by reading those chapters. It is after the meaning of all those passages that God intended the promise of His covenant, "I will be a God to thee, and to thy seed after thee," of which circumcision was the appointed token; which also we have seen was, like baptism, administered but once; like it was the external means of admission into the Church of the Messiah. We have seen also its correspondence with baptism in its spiritual signification as an emblematical ordinance in representing the purification of the soul from sin by divine grace, and the service of God to be in newness or holiness of life. And we have seen it administered by divine appointment to Abraham after he had become a believer, but to his posterity in their early infancy, on account of their relationship to him, and the promise in relation to his seed after him.

From all this, if

GOD STILL ACTS ON THE SAME PRINCIPLES,

if those passages in the Psalms, Proverbs, Isaiah, etc., etc., are still true—one would reasonably expect—to cheer and encourage the hearts of his people now, who love their children as dearly, in regard to their highest interests, as those of old, as well as to deepen in their minds, and in their children's, the corresponding sense of responsibility, considering their privileged condition—that He would also use the ordinance of baptism for their children to indicate the truth, as precious now as ever it was—that "The mercy of the Lord is from everlasting to everlasting upon them that fear Him, and His righteousness unto children's children." "The children of thy servants shall continue, and their seed shall be established before thee." That is, "I will be a God unto thee, and to thy seed after thee." It certainly would be as consistent with propriety to represent this precious truth by baptism as it was to do the same thing before by the other corresponding ordinance of circumcision. That it has been so appointed, I have proven to you at length by one very strong line of proof, the established fact that immediately after the apostles had retired, infants were being baptized throughout the length and breadth of the Church, as by apostolic authority. Our Baptist friends rely on this kind of argument as *their* PROOF conclusive of the first day of the week being the Lord's day and Sabbath, which is also a more important institution. They cannot, therefore, with propriety reject it on infant-baptism. Their disposition to treat it in that way shows they feel its force as powerful. And the distortions, concealments, and gross misrepresentations they practice in connection with the evidence of history, such as I have brought to your view, shows very clearly their consciousness that *their* cause could not prevail by dealing fairly and honestly with that evidence. In harmony with that practice everywhere at the close of the apostolic age, we have seen, also, under Paul's personal superintendence, the household of Lydia baptized along with herself upon her becoming a believer, no faith in their case being hinted.

BAPTISTS MAKE A STRONG OBJECTION,

however, to this last sentence, in what is said of Paul and Silas, after they left the Philippine jail (Acts xvi. 34, 36, 40). Pengilly states it thus (p. 38), "'They entered the house of Lydia,' (for my reader will remember this was the only other Christian house in the city, and in this family the only other persons baptized); and here undoubtedly, they would meet with her 'household,' which they had baptized; having entered, we read, 'when they had seen THE BRETHREN, they COMFORTED THEM, and departed.' If, then, Lydia's *household be* denominated 'brethren,' and were capable of being 'comforted,' by the Word, they must have been BELIEVERS IN CHRIST." So important and decisive does Pengilly desire this proof to be felt that he has the principal expressions in capital letters. Well, looking at the above, as he states it, it seems unanswerable to the contrary. For, for all that appears in the whole chapter, or elsewhere, Lydia's seems to have been "the only other Christian house in the city." And by the term, "brethren" there, I have no doubt fellow-*believers* are meant. The next *fact* is, her family were "the only other persons baptized;" also, in her house Paul and Silas "would meet with her household" may at once be admitted. The last step in the reasoning is, "If, then, Lydia's household be denominated brethren, and were capable of being comforted by the Word, they *must have been* believers in Christ." Well, if that IF at the beginning of the last sentence is admitted, as proposed, I admit the conclusion is correct. "But, what?" I hear Pengilly saying by implication, "do you doubt it, when it is as clear as day that Lydia's household were denominated brethren? You are not honest nor willing to see the plainest truth, if you doubt that, and are determined to hold by infant-baptism at all costs." I have here described what a Baptist will admit, on reading it, to be his own impression of the matter, and Pengilly's and other Baptist teachers' reasoning on our unbelief. But I have *some reason* for my doubt, notwithstanding, which you will never find whispered to Baptists in their books, etc., and it is very accessible; and their leaders, at least, cannot say they have not noticed it, as they have seen it pointed out to them by our side. But before giving it, allow me to say I have waited so long here to show you, brethren, how, in the Scriptures, as well as in Early Church History, and quotations from Paedobaptists, Baptist writers make strong, and to their readers, apparently conclusive statements, which, when examined by those who take the trouble of looking into the matters for themselves, and have understanding, turn out, as I will show you of this one, to be the offspring of ignorance, or proselytizing dishonesty, or both.

Now, first, it is said Lydia's household were denominated "brethren." Let us look again at the passage (ver. 40), "And they went out of the prison, and entered into the house of Lydia; and when they had seen the brethren, they comforted them and departed." What is really said is that they had "been the brethren," not that the household of Lydia were called the brethren. O but, says Pengilly, etc., it comes to the same thing. Paul and Silas had left the Phillippine jailer and his family, and came to Lydia's house. Lydia's house "was the only other Christian house in the city (of Phillippi), and she and her household "the only other persons baptized;" therefore (they reason and affirm) her household alone were the only brethren Paul and Silas could "see" and "comfort" on the occasion, for there were no other Christians in the city. These statements are positive enough, and the proof should be quite decisive. But let us see for ourselves. In the preceding chapter (Acts xv. 40) we read of Paul and Silas beginning their journey towards Phillippi. Then, immediately after, (chap. xvi. 1 and 3) of Timotheus joining them. Again, it is admitted by all that Luke was the writer of the "Acts" (on which see Luke i. 3; Acts i. 1), and he speaks of himself as also with them. For, in describing their proceedings, before they came to Philippi, and within it, he often uses the words "we" and "us" (chap. xvi. ver. 10, 11, 12, 13, 14, 15, 16, 17), which, of course, includes the writer himself. Examine from the first to the fourteenth verse of that chapter, as also onwards, and you will see these two "brethren" accompanied Paul and Silas. Timothy is again specified as with them after they had left Philippi (xvii. 15). In chapter xvi. 17, after Lydia's baptism is mentioned, Luke says of the damsel possessed of a spirit of divination, "The same followed Paul and *us*," in which Paul is distinguished from the "us," and "us" being plural, denotes more than the writer. Now, as Pengilly says, Lydia's was it appears, the only Christian house at this time in the city besides the jailor's. Also, at the time of her baptism, we read (ver. 15), "She besought us, saying, If ye have judged me to be faithful to the Lord, COME INTO MY HOUSE AND ABIDE THERE. And she *constrained us.*" That is, they all made their abode in her house. Again, it is plain that only Paul and Silas were taken to the prison (ver. 19, 25, 29, 40). Therefore, their two brethren, Timotheus and Luke, were not with them there, but abiding with Lydia. Hence, when they again entered Lydia's house they would see THESE "BRETHREN," their companions and fellow-labourers, who would be "comforted" by seeing them again free, after the abuse of many bloody stripes they had seen them receive, etc., (ver. 23, 33), and by hearing from them of God's grace to the jailer and his family. Now, all this is easily perceivable in the narrative within the chapter. What, then, shall we think now, when we see the real facts, of the Baptist affirmation, that 'Lydia's household were the only Christians Paul and Silas could see and comfort outside of the jail. No others in the city. Therefore, these must have been believers themselves when baptized with her.' Yes, and although the incorrectness of this has been shown by Infant Baptists, and the evident untruthfulness of all this is "as plain as day;" yet in their Publication Society books, and by ministers, and others, they still repeat the same thing, without reference to these plain facts at all. This, brethren, is inherent in the nature of their cause. It is not of God, and, therefore, not truth, but untruth suits it best.

It is not my intention to go into the whole subject as I have not limits or time. But I am showing you that there is *Scriptural* authority for the doctrine and administration in question. Let me notice another example, namely that of

THE PHILIPPINE JAILER AND HIS HOUSEHOLD,

(Same chapter, ver. 33, 34), "And he took them the same hour of the night and washed their stripes; and was, *baptized*, HE AND ALL HIS *straightway*. And when he had brought them into his house, he set meat before them and rejoiced, believing in God, with all his house." Here you observe it is distinctly said " all his " were baptized with him at once. From the fact, however, that " all his house " are said to have rejoiced with him, and, as may *seem*, to have also believed with him, Baptists affirm they were capable of faith and were believers, therefore no infant was baptized; as also from the statement (ver. 32), that Paul spake the word " to *all* that were in his house." Now supposing they all had faith there would be no proof in that against baptism of infants, as it is not said or hinted that it was refused an infant. It is quite true, of course, a parent when converted may not have infant children. Yet still the children he has may be legitimately baptizable on account of their parent's faith, just as, while infants were circumcised, so were those more advanced in years on account of Abraham's faith, (Gen. xvii. 13, 14, 23-27).

But we don't agree from what is said of the family that it follows there was no infant present or baptized. To state that the Apostle spoke the word " to all in the house " would mean in the common style of Scripture, ' all capable of understanding it,' without implying there was no child present too young for that; and similarly of the expression " all " in verse 34. All those rejoiced who were capable of that emotion and no more. And in verse 33, all capable of being baptized were baptized; but a babe can be baptized, as that is an act done to the child not necessarily implying its understanding any more than circumcision. We don't say this in proof of a child being present, but that there might have been one.

But let us hear Pengilly. He says (p. 40) on this passage (ver. 34). " Then it follows he had no infant children or those words cannot include them ; for of this faith they would be incapable." In support of this statement he gives the following quotation from Matthew Henry's Commentary on this passage, namely, " The voice of rejoicing with that of salvation was heard in the jailer's house. *He rejoiced, believing in God.* There was NONE in his house that refused to be baptized, and so made a jar in the CEREMONY, but *they were unanimous* in embracing the gospel, which added much to the joy." Now brethren,

PENGILLY HERE AGAIN MISQUOTES M. HENRY TWICE, AND TOTALLY MISREPRERENTS HIM.

Observe that word, "ceremony." I have Matthew Henry's Commentary open before me, and the word is NOT "ceremony" there, but HARMONY, a quite different word. And notice, further, Pengilly stops his quotation as above, but Henry goes on thus, " OR, IT MAY BE READ, *He, believing in God,* rejoiced all the house over; *panoika*—he went to every apartment, expressing his joy." Now, why did Pengilly not add that other short sentence ? If he had, it would appear that Henry admitted the Greek might, in his opinion, be taken fairly to mean the latter translation, and that he would not speak decidedly of either. This Pengilly neither gives nor hints at, but presents the first way as his decided opinion; which is, of course, a deliberate misrepresentation, as he could not quote the one portion without seeing the other. Again, the expression of Henry, "there was none in the house that REFUSED to be baptized," does not, after all, imply that the jailer "had no infant-children" baptized. Such an expression could only be used by Henry, or any other of adults who might personally refuse; but a babe, certainly, would never refuse or dissent. So that the quotation from Henry, though he gave no other reading, does not exclude infants, as Pengilly wishes his readers to think. BUT THIS IS NOT ALL, brethren. Note the following, which was also before Pengilly's eyes. On the last clause of verse 31st, Henry says:—" The extension of this to his (the jailer's) family: *Thou shalt be saved and thy house*; that is, 'God will be in Christ a God to thee and to thy seed, as He was to Abraham. . . Those of thy HOUSE THAT ARE INFANTS shall be *admitted* into the visible church *with thee.* and thereby put in a fair way for salvation, those that are grown up shall have the means of salvation brought to them,'" etc. What shall I more say ? Nor is this the only case I have shown you of Pengilly's gross misrepresentation of Henry (see p. 26-29).

Lastly on this case. There is in verse 34 decisive proof that this family were baptized

ON ACCOUNT OF THEIR PARENTS' FAITH.

The question as to whether they literally all had faith or not does not affect this point. It stands out by itself, a proof of what we affirm, which ever way the other may be, as in Lydia's case. It lies in the Greek word rendered "believing." Baptist writers don't deny the correctness of what I am going to show you, but with their own readers and audiences they simply say nothing of this, who therefore don't know of it. They make out the household's faith from their joy, and the form of the sentence about believing in our English version, which is obscure, from the nature of our language in translation of some Greek expressions; and they next seek to exclude infants by quotations from Pædobaptists, as Matthew Henry, to make him, etc., say, what he has said the opposite of. As I have shown you now in a large number of cases they take care that their readers will not learn the real facts.

Our English language has several peculiarities different from *all* other languages :—Latin, Greek, Hebrew, German, French, Gaelic, etc. Among other things this is so in regard to

THE SINGULAR AND PLURAL NUMBERS

of certain parts of speech. Our nouns, for instance, have a different form in the singular and plural, as "man, men," "child, children," "sky, skies." We never use 'men' for a 'man,' nor a 'child' for 'children.' But our adjectives and participles never thus change their form. Thus in "*bright* sky, *bright* skies," 'bright' is the same in both, and not "brights" in the plural; and in "the letter was *written*, the letters were *written*," the word 'written' is also the same; but 'letters' is the plural of 'letter,' and 'were' that of 'was.' Now in other languages ancient and modern, the words for 'bright' and 'written' would be altered to correspond with the others, just as universally as our nouns and pronouns are altered. And so of all other corresponding parts of speech. Thus, *Bonus* vir (Latin) is, '*good* man,' but, *boni* viri, '*good* men;' likewise (Greek) *agathos* anthropos, in singular, *agathoi* anthropoi, in plural; (German) *guter* mann, *gute* männer, mean the same respectively, viz., good man, good men. Again, the Latin words, credens Deo, 'believing God,' can be used and understood of *only* one person; but creden*tes* Deo, *always* means more than one person 'believing God,' while in the

English, the word 'believing,' is not altered a letter whether we speak of one or more persons. The plural of the Latin 'credens' you see is formed by changing its "s" at the end into "tes." Now let us apply this to the case in hand, for in Greek it is precisely the same. The Greek word "*pepisteukos*" is the perfect tense, participle, masculine gender, singular number, of the verb 'to believe,' is used of one person alone, and signifies literally "he having believed." But when more than one person is referred to as believing, the form '*pepisteukotes*,' the plural being formed by changing the 's' at the end of the singular into 'tes,' just as in the Latin, 'credens, credentes.' This rule, understand, is constant as much for example as in our English 'he' and 'they.' You would never understand several persons by '*he* said' so and so, nor only one person by, '*they* rejoiced.' Now I will set before you the Greek words of verse 34, in their precise order in the Greek Testament. They are "anagagon te autous eis ton oikon autou, paretheke trapezan, kai ēgalliasato panoiki PEPISTEUKOS TO THEO." The words in small capitals are the terms under present consideration. In the Baptist version of the New Testament it is rendered thus, "And having brought them up into his house, he set food before them, and rejoiced with all his house, *believing in God*." A common English reader, unacquainted with the Greek, would be at a loss in a critical examination of this for the precise meaning, whether to connect the, "with all his house," immediately with the "and rejoiced," or with, "believing in God;" thus, "and rejoiced with all his house, he having believed in God;" or, "and rejoiced, all his house believing in God with himself." This arises from the obscurity of the English word "believing," from its having the same form in our singular and plural. Now suppose the Greek words at the end to have been "pepisteuko*tes* to theo;" then the rendering would necessarily be, "and he rejoiced with all his house, they having believed in God;" meaning the jailer and his household, or the household considered by themselves. But *in point of fact* the Greek participle IS SINGULAR, referring so far as its meaning and reference extends to but one person, masculine gender. 'The obscurity becomes removed by translating it literally, "and rejoiced with all his house, he having believed in God." Now no one can say that this is not the literal translation. And the Baptist Version gives the words in precisely the same order. The quotation from Matthew Henry by the way (p. 109), in each of the two readings he gives of the passage, translates the faith as the jailer's not theirs, so far as that word speaks, thus (1) He rejoiced, believing in God, etc., (2) Or it may be read, *He believing in God*, rejoiced, etc." So far then as faith is *affirmed* of any, it is only affirmed of one, and that evidently the father of the household. So here is the baptism of a parent and his household together on his becoming a believer, which is pointed out distinctly as the occasion by the Holy Spirit. The absence of such a specification of faith of the household if they had faith, seems to mean to teach us that that in them was not necessary to entitle them to baptism, for were it otherwise, it could have been specified by writing the plural participle to include them rather than the singular one which could not include more than the parent in its meaning. Lastly, it seems clear that they rejoiced with him, or he with them. But it is said that, that implies faith in them. Well if it did it did so in his case as well, yet the Holy Spirit did not think it sufficient to leave it to be inferred in his case, but besides stating his joy says that HE believed. There was of course special reason for that distinction in his case and its absence from theirs. But I have to add further, it is not difficult to see after all that

THEIR GREAT JOY DOES NOT PROVE THEY HAD FAITH

in Christ themselves. Faith brings joy, but different causes produce similar effects. They saw their father a very short time before wretched, and trembling for his life, and his soul, and the earthquake, etc., at that midnight hour would, in addition, have disturbed their own minds. Between the excitement from apprehension of personal impending danger and concern at their parent's condition, whom they loved, and in whose life and welfare also their own was so much bound up, it would be no small cause of joy itself to see the sword safely sheathed again, that was on the point of entering his heart by his own hand, and a father in agony under the apprehension of the wrath of God—to see all his darkness and fears dispelled by the light that dawned upon his soul, changing his distress into the sweetest peace and joy unspeakable, and full of glory, making him, we may suppose from what we read of him, like the man in the third chapter (ver. 1–11), for a less mercy, leaping and praising God. Now, we know that these were the facts. Hence it is not *necessary* to suppose faith in them. The circumstances would fully account for it without it. But, notice the structure of the expression— "he having believed in God," seems from its position, after stating his and their joy, to be given as the reason of that, joy in their case and his. It was HIS faith. It came first, then followed all the other things—his washing the apostles stripes, his being baptized by them with all his straightway, bringing them into his house, giving them food, and with all and through all, happy, very happy, his family feeling the influence of the joyful change from natural affection alone, as well as relief from the fears of the awful night's experiences. Never did they see their parent so wretched before, nor so happy as now. What family would not rejoice in such circumstances as those?

We have explained, now, TWO DISTINCT EXAMPLES, under the personal administration of the inspired apostle, and recorded by the inspired historian, Luke, of households baptized as such on occasion of the parent's faith, and having that as the only revealed reason. And "the things which are revealed belong to us and to our children for ever." (Deut. xxix. 29).

Besides these there are other households, but let these suffice at present for my purpose. I next note in the present connection

THE SAVIOUR'S TESTIMONY ABOUT THE INFANTS:

"And they brought to him also INFANTS, that he might touch them; and, the disciples, seeing it, REBUKED them. But, Jesus, calling them to him, said, "Suffer the little children to come to me, and forbid them not; for to such belongs the kingdom of God." "And they brought little children to him, that he might touch them; and the disciples rebuked those who brought them. But Jesus, seeing it, WAS MUCH DISPLEASED, and said to them: Suffer the little children to come to me; forbid them not; for to such belongs the Kingdom of God." (Luke xviii. 15, 16;

Mark x. 13, 14—Baptist Version). Many, when they hear the words, "kingdom of God," "kingdom of heaven," never think they have any other reference than the kingdom of glory *in* heaven above. Whereas, in Scripture, and particularly in the Saviour's lips, they are a most frequent name of his Church below, which is the kingdom of God—of heaven on earth, of which himself, the God and sovereign of heaven, is the acknowledged king, the laws and blessings heavenly, and, to all, in the possession of its gracious privileges who look to Jesus, and serve God in him according to the divine instruction of those privileges, and the means of receiving grace they afford, there is the assured prospect to each one of them of hearing the call from him who sits between the cherubim, over the mercy-seat, sprinkled with Jesus' blood, to come up higher, and of being translated to heaven and its eternal blessedness and weight of glory! The great appropriateness of those names of the church of Christ it is easy to perceive, as also to see them often applied to it. (Matt. iii. 2; iv. 17; v. 19; xi. 12; xii. 28; xiii. 21, 31, 33, 44, 45, 47, 52; xx. 1; xxii. 2; xxv. 1; Mark i. 15; Luke x. 9, 11; xi. 20, etc., etc.) Now, in the passages just quoted about the infants brought by others to Jesus for his blessing, unconsciously to the little ones themselves, we see the Saviour's heart in much favour of it; and how he felt towards his disciples for their improper opposition. This last part is also very instructive. The disciples were, no doubt, zealous, but as yet they had not much of the Spirit, and did not understand aright the economy, genius, spirit, and way of his kingdom; yet, notwithstanding all their lesser privileges, compared with those they had afterwards, and those we now have, "He was sore displeased" at THEIR standing in the way on the occasion, and "*rebuked* THEM." It is pleasant to observe they never afterwards did the like; but sad that the record by inspiration of that "sore" displeasure and rebuke for the information of his disciples in all ages, is by some disregarded.

There is no reason whatever for limiting the meaning of his words, "for of such is the kingdom of God," to heaven above only. It is true, there is such in the kingdom above, as we find elsewhere indicated (Psalms viii. 2, etc.); and it is just as true such had, and have, a place in that on earth; namely, those of parents in whose heart by divine grace, there is the desire to bring them to Jesus for his blessing, even his baptism with the holy Spirit. (John i. 33). He is so much in favour of such being brought to him, as, among other means, to require it to be represented and done in his church in baptism, before all, as a perpetual ordinance, that it may be always before parents' eyes for their encouragement, and children's likewise; that they may know assuredly he does not overlook them, but is VERY *tenderly* interested in them, and wishes them to come to him, and be brought while the very earliest dew of their youth is upon them. How very suggestive of this also are the statements of the Holy Ghost in

1. CORINTH. vii. 14,

" For the unbelieving husband is sanctified by the [believing] wife, and the unbelieving wife is sanctified by the [believing] husband: else were your children unclean; BUT NOW ARE THEY HOLY."

These words in capitals, I need not say to you, brethren, were written by God himself, as much as any other portion of his Word. The children of a believing parent, as soon as they become children, that is, as soon as they are born, ARE HOLY. How do I know? God says it distinctly before our eyes. And also that the children of unbelieving parents are quite the opposite, " UNCLEAN," that is, NOT HOLY. Now, these words represent actual conditions, evidently meant to be understood by us as of great moment. The term HOLY, and its opposite in God's lips, are no light or indifferent matters, whatever sense is legitimately to be attached to them. We are to attach the sense in which He uses them, and the value, the importance as well; no more, NO LESS. It is admitted that these children when born are not holy *in spirit*, but conceived in sin and shapen in iniquity, and, as all believers were, have a heart at enmity with God in its depravity, and are, " by nature, the children of wrath even as others." They need all to be born again before they will be holy in spirit. That, then, is not the holiness God affirms of them. There IS, however, another sense in which he often uses this term. The tabernacle, temple, the sacrifices, the vessels of the sanctuary, etc., were said by him to be "holy," and being material altogether, were not spiritually holy; but they were appointed by him, and consequently set apart by his people, and consecrated by his direction for his religious service. Also the *whole* Jewish people, from the infants to the aged, were " holy" to the Lord *in this sense* as distinguished from the other nations of men, though they were not all holy in spirit and life. We know when they were in the wilderness under Moses, they were far from that, yet the Lord said to them, then, " Thou art an holy people unto the Lord thy God: the Lord thy God hath chosen thee to be a special people unto himself, above all people that are upon the face of the earth." " Thou shalt, therefore keep the commandments which I command thee this day." (Deut. vi. 6, 10). At the same time, he declared that they were holy to him in the first sense in order that they might become so in the other and higher sense; "And the Lord hath avouched thee this day to be his peculiar people, as he hath promised thee, and that thou shouldest keep all his commandments; and to make thee high above all nations which he hath made in praise, and in name, and in honour; and that THOU MAYEST BE an holy people unto the Lord thy God, as he hath spoken." (Deut. xxvi. 19.) In these places and many others we find a divine sense of the term " holy," to denote the favoured condition of the children of Israel as the children of Abraham, Isaac, and Jacob, and his choice and separation of them among mankind for his ordinances, service, and blessings that make truly rich—" *Thou art* an holy people unto the Lord. . . . He hath chosen thee to be a special people to himself, . . . in order *that* thou mayest be a holy people," etc. This, there can be no reasonable doubt, is the meaning of the word in 1 Cor. vii. 14. It has reference to the covenant that still contains in its terms, " The seed of the righteous shall be blessed after him. The mercy of the Lord is from everlasting to everlasting upon them that fear him, and his righteousness unto children's children." These and all the others are God's words to us still, of them that fear him. That being so, it is plain the children of such are holy in the very same sense, and for the very same ends as the chosen race were of old. For " the thoughts of his heart endure to all generations." (Ps. xxxiii. 11). This still further appears by the contrast God himself intimates in the position of the children of unbelievers. They are unclean, unholy. The special promises in regard to the seed of the righteous imply that the others are not so favoured. But God speaks plainly, and often to that effect. For instance, in the Second Commandment (Exod. 20), "visiting the iniquity of the fathers upon the children unto the third and fourth generation of them that hate me"—"upon the children, and upon the children's children." (xxxiv. 7.) "The seed of the wicked shall be cut off." "Their fruit shall thou destroy from the earth, and their seed from among the children of men." (Psalms xxxvii. 28; xxi. 10.) "Thou shewest loving-kindness unto thousands, and recompensest the iniquity of the fathers into the bosom of their children after them: the Great, the Mighty God, the Lord of hosts is his name." (Jerem. xxxii. 18.)

The doctrine of the passage we are considering, then, appears to be that where even only one of the parents, and that either the father or the mother, is a believer, God's purpose is that his or her relation to himself by faith in Christ will so sanctify the marriage relation with the other unbelieving parent, with regard to the offspring, that they will occupy the same position in his eyes, and gracious dealings as those whose parents both trust in, love, worship, and serve Him as their God. The evil of the relation of the children to an unbelieving parent will be graciously overborne by his favour towards the believing parent, whose heaven-born and very tender yearnings for the salvation of his or her offspring he is disposed in this way to regard. Hence, such also are to receive the Covenant Promise, as made to them. For this reason, no doubt, he expressed it in the singular number, "I will be a God to *thee* and to *thy* seed after thee." "I will pour my spirit upon *thy* seed, and my blessing on *thine* offspring."

But before leaving this passage I must place before you

THE BAPTIST INTERPRETATION OF 1 COR. VII., 14.

They make the term "holy" to signify "lawful or legitimate children," not born as of "fornication or adultery." And the other term "unclean" to mean "illegitimate children" or bastards. Cramp, in his Catechism (p. 73-75), says, "this is the *common sense* interpretation of the text, and is now generally acquiesced in by commentators." By this last sentence his readers will be led to suppose, what he no doubt intends, that the commentators of all the denominations "generally" acquiesce in this view. This is simply and very untrue. Dr. Carson says, "it is usually and sufficiently explained" in this way, that is to say, 'by Baptists.' That you may see that I will fairly exhibit their reasoning on it, I will first give you what Carson their great leader says (p. 208) in his own words; as follows:—"With respect to the passage referred to, (1 Cor. vii., 14.) it is usually and sufficiently explained, by an allusion to Ezra x., 3, 44; Neh. xiii., 23, 24. The sanctification referred to MUST be *legitimacy according to the law of God.* Such marriages were not lawful to the Jews, and both the wives and their children were put away. It is the duty of the disciples to marry in the Lord; but even if they transgress that law, OR ARE CONVERTED AFTER MARRIAGE, they are not like the Jews, to put away their wives and children on repentance. The marriage is to continue, and the relation is sanctified, just as their food is sanctified or blessed to their use. Now this is an important—a most important thing. As JESUS COMMANDS HIS DISCIPLES to marry in the Lord, HAD NO PROVISION been made, every marriage contrary to this, must be given up on repentance, JUST AS FORNICATION and ADULTERY; and the *offspring* of such marriages could *not* be considered as the children of *marriage*, according to God's institution. It is said in reply to this, that even the marriages of UNBELIEVERS are LAWFUL, and the *offspring* LEGITIMATE. Certainly—because they are according to the law both of God and man. But as Christ commands his people to marry in the Lord, to marry otherwise IS CONTRARY TO GOD'S LAW. Neither such marriage, then, nor the offspring of it would be legitimate according to the law of God, except by this provision. The marriage might be legitimate according to the law of man, and the children legitimate according to the law of man, but neither would be legitimate according to the law of God. This provision then is most bountiful and kind. The believer, by remaining in his marriage with the unbeliever, does not continue in sin, as he would by continuing in fornication. His marriage is sanctified to him. I can see NO DIFFICULTY in the passage."

This is the usual or rather the universal Baptist exposition of this passage, who all see no difficulty in it. But let us see for ourselves. According to it, then, such a marriage, consummated contrary to Christ's command, is contrary to God's law; therefore it and its issue are as illegitimate as fornication or adultery and its issue, in the judgment of that law and of Christ, the lawgiver; who still forbids such marriage, on the same grounds.

The next fact alleged is, that the *same* marriage union as soon as consummated is "lawful" and its offspring "legitimate" according to the same law of God and Christ, the lawgiver. Here two direct CONTRADICTIONS seem to be affirmed. There is a reason given for the legitimacy, which we will look at immediately. Meanwhile, apart from it, Jesus is represented first as always commanding his disciples before they marry not to marry an unbeliever, and on this ground such a marriage and its offspring would be "illegitimate." But that the moment a wayward disciple disobediently does form such a union, Jesus then says of the same thing: It is a quite lawful marriage and its offspring are as "legitimate" as those of my people who have conformed to my command to marry "only in the Lord."

The reason of this, we are told, is given in this passage, "The unbelieving husband is sanctified by the (believing) wife." "The sanctification referred to" here, says Carson, "must be *legitimacy* according to the law of God." Well, the reason of that sanctification of the unbelieving partner "by" the other as a believer seems evidently the faith of the believing one, as faith is the question at issue as the deciding quality in the case. And again, the reason of Christ's command to his disciples not to marry an unbeliever, is evidently the same, the one has not faith, while the other has. It is admitted by Carson that the marriage of two UNBELIEVERS and their offspring are "legitimate" from the first, there being no prohibition of such. For it is "according to the law both of God and man." Here, then, are two things: THE FAITH of His disciple (by which he becomes a disciple), IS THE REASON why Jesus commands him not to marry one who has not faith, as his marriage (according to Carson) would, in that case, become to him an unlawful marriage, " contrary to the law of God," and his children " bastards." And again, THE SAME FAITH in the SAME PERSON is THE REASON of that union, if entered into in disobedience of Christ's prohibition, becoming a lawful marriage, or one in accordance with God's law and Christ's will; while yet, again, the Lord still continues to declare to his unmarried people that such a marriage for them is ILLEGITIMATE, contrary to God's law, etc.

But further, the passage refers not merely to a believer who, as such, may have married an unbeliever. That question is really not referred to in particular at all. There were many at that time married before they were converted, whose husbands or wives still remained heathens. This epistle of Paul was written about five years only after the gospel had been preached first at Corinth. The passage specially contemplates those who were heathens when they were married, but now were Christians, their husband or wife not being so. How then will the Baptist exposition fit into this? Carson admits that the passage applies to such as "are converted after their marriage." Well, he admits the marriage of two unbelievers, as such, and their offspring to be legitimate. That is, while both unbelievers at the time and afterwards, no sin was chargeable on either of them on that account. But a gracious change takes place in one of them into a believer in Jesus; the other, however, remains as before. The children were all legitimate before. Do they become illegitimate now? Has the new-born faith of the wife that effect, transforming what was *legitimate* into illegitimacy, declaring what was in accordance with God's law not to have been so? It seems rather to have had quite a different kind of effect,—for Paul says to the believing parent that the other was sanctified by her; "else were your children unclean; but now are they holy." We cannot dwell longer to show other things. In short, the apostle is not speaking of illegitimate children at all. For they were legitimate, as the children of lawful marriage; but now by the faith of one parent their condition is greatly altered for the *better*, as being among those whom God favours, in being made the subjects of that parent's prayers, etc., etc., and coming within the range of the covenant promise. This is the exposition that fits into the words completely, and harmonizes with much we see all throughout the Scriptures.

How Carson could see no difficulty in his way of it, and how Baptists constantly teach it as clear and satisfactory, can only be explained by the reason we have seen operating so much in other connections—special pleading. I may add that this Baptist exposition is just the same in *nature* with Rome's doctrine that no heretics are truly married; that conversion to and marriage by Rome alone is consistent with legitimacy.

I have endeavoured to set before you that precious covenant of mercy God makes not only with his people themselves, but embracing in its gracious purposes the offspring parental affection so much regards, and to show this, among other things, he desires that precious truth impressed on our minds by the ordinance of baptism soon after they are born into the world, and in the case of a parent converted from heathenism, that then ' he and all his ' will be baptized straightway.

I need not tell you, however, that we don't believe that the admission of children by baptism into the number of the visible church of God on earth implies also to them, as Baptists say,

A RIGHT TO THE LORD'S SUPPER,

and all the privileges of membership in full communion. Those who speak so forget that nothing of all this is a matter of right, but is all of grace. Besides, the second ordinance is quite different in important respects from the former. In the former, the person is acted UPON, is baptized by another, not by himself, which can be done with the youngest age, as in circumcision, or as the infants were taken up and blessed by Jesus, when he said, "Suffer little children to come unto me, and forbid them not; for of such is the kingdom of God." In fact the bringing of their little ones, one by one, to the sanctuary for baptism, by pious parents, from pious affection and desire toward God that he would baptize them himself with his Spirit from on high, would wash them in the blood of Jesus and convert them to himself, is really in its NATURE, A PRAYER to God that he would do these things for them; which can all be done any day after birth so far as age is concerned, the same as prayer offered for them.

In the Lord's Supper it is altogether different. The Passover to which it corresponds was not partaken of by Jewish children before twelve years of age (Luke ii., 42). In it they *acted* personally with regard to the objects of the ordinance (Exod. xii., 26, etc.) All persons were liable to be refused participation in the Passover though circumcised, as for doing "ought presumptuously" (Numb. xv., 30), and not observing their duties (Exod. xii., 15; 19; Lev. vii., 20–27), while their discipline on drunkenness, blasphemy, adultery, etc., went further than now (Deut. xxi., 20; Lev. xx., 10; xxiv., 16). In like manner two things are necessary for the Lord's Supper—namely, AGE ENOUGH for intelligent discernment of the Lord's body and blood in the emblems, and for personal commemoration of him in the showing forth of his death. And second, the possession of faith in Christ that worketh by love, as implied, for instance, in the direction—"But let a man examine himself, and so let him eat of that bread and drink of that cup. For he that eateth and drinketh unworthily eateth and drinketh judgment to himself." Till then (for baptism by water does not regenerate) it is the duty as it is the wisdom of the baptized to strive to enter in at the strait gate. When they have received the higher baptism, with its faith and love, and hungering and thirsting after righteousness and grace, then, with much joyful welcome can they take and eat the bread and drink the cup of blessing in remembrance of him. Meanwhile they have till then no voice in the management of the church's affairs and responsibilities any more than the sons and daughters of Baptist families who are not members of their church. But they are the special subjects of its instructions, its prayers, and its cares. As when the Lord said to Peter, "Feed my lambs. Feed my sheep. Feed my sheep" (John xxi., 15–17), he gave a place, and a prominent place, to the "lambs" of the 'flock,'—"MY lambs," that they might be brought up in the nurture and admonition of the Lord" (Ephes. vi., 4).

I have got two points to speak on and then close this section of my subject, viz., the extent of the covenant promise in relation to the offspring, and the principle on which its fulfilment proceeds. Both are very important, therefore I wish to speak on them. The first of these questions is

THE EXTENT OF THE COVENANT PROMISE.

Now, suppose the words had been thus, "I will be a God to thee and to ALL thy seed after thee." "I will pour my spirit upon ALL thy seed, and my blessing upon ALL thine offspring." "The promise is to you and to ALL your children." In that case the meaning would clearly be that *all* the children of believing parents would receive the Spirit in large measure, and that the Lord would be their God as he was their parents, none at all being excepted. But the words don't go so far, but are, "I will be a God to thee and to *thy seed* after thee." Hence, it appears that the Covenant Promise does not necessarily extend to all their offspring, according to the words; while it appears otherwise, that "ALL" is not meant. Yet, the Lord's command to Abraham *as to the extent of the* SIGN of that covenant was (Exod. xvii. 10, 14), "EVERY man child among you shall be circumcised. And the uncircumcised man child, whose flesh of his foreskin is not circumcised, that soul shall be cut off from his people; he hath broken my covenant." Hence, we read that Ishmael was circumcised with his father, although he became a *wild* man; his hand against every man, and every man's against him (Genes. xvi. 21); and the covenant was made good only in Isaac. Then, of *his* seed, Esau and Jacob, one was taken and the other left (Rom. ix. 6–16.) Absalom was the son of David, the sweet singer of Israel, the man after God's own heart; yet, at his death, no doubt from the well-founded belief of his being lost forever, we hear David crying out in anguish, " Would God I had died for thee, O Absalom, my son, my son!" This being so, some may think, Where, then, is the value of the covenant as to the offspring? We may be sure God does not use these and like words to raise great hope in his people's hearts in regard to their children without solid reason. There is much value in it (Rom. iii. 1, 2.)

The children as such of ungodly parents are not, we have seen, in the same favoured condition as those of believers; yet, blessed be God's name, he does not withhold his salvation altogether from such. We see sons and daughters of godless fathers and mothers brought to the knowledge of the truth as it is in Jesus. And when, for example, the gospel is brought to the heathen and Romanists, by the grace of God many are converted whose parents were without God for the preceding generations. Yet, while this is so, as we are very glad to know, still his rule is to raise up a seed in each generation to serve him, chiefly from the children of his people. Take, of your own acquaintances, or of history, any number of really pious parents, and the same number of ungodly parents, and consider the children as a whole of the one and the other class, and it will be seen that much fewer become pious and God-fearing from among those whose parents had not his fear before their eyes, than of those whose fathers or mothers, or both parents, delight themselves in God, and constantly plead with him for them, and day by day, year after year, are found carefully 'training them up in the way they should go,' to which the hopeful promise is made. (Prov. xxii. 6.) While God is sovereign in his grace, bestowing it as he pleases, and informs us that all regenerated by him are "born, not of blood, nor of the will of the flesh, nor of the will of man, but of God" (John i. 13); yet he follows general rules of procedure, and bestows rewards of grace on them that seek him for themselves and others, and in connection with those appointed means they use with him, and towards themselves and others. And as with the godly (only with them) the love of their children leads them to be most earnest about their salvation, next to their own, so, according to the divine procedure, their children will be more visited with grace from above unto everlasting life than other families without pious parents, not so instructed, prayed for, and brought up, which will usually remain, in consequence, without being favoured from above in the same way.

From these unquestionable facts we can see in the very fact of such children being born, by God's act, of godly parents who will so love and act towards and for them, that they from their birth (though sinful and hell-deserving) are the subjects of special privileges pertaining to salvation in a sense and to an extent that others *in the nature of their* position are not. If God declares, and acts accordingly, which we know from all experience he does, that the outpouring of his spirit unto salvation upon men in general will be in connection with the means of grace employed towards them by his own believing people, and in answer to their prayers to Himself; so that those among whom they do not live at all, or do not bring the word of life to, nor pray for, there irreligion, indifference to God and salvation will usually continue to abound unbroken, and souls all be perishing; on the other hand, that where his people bring the gospel, and labour with all prayer and supplication in the Spirit, there will God be found of them that sought him not, and they that were hitherto not his people will become the children of the living God (Rom. ix. 24–26; x. 14–17); if God does so among mankind in general, will he not act on the same principles in regard to the children of believers? But such children are EVER WITH THEIR PARENTS, are continually taught by them the word of life, and are always prayed for every day of their lives, with Christian zeal and earnestness, *quickened* and *increased* by all the FORCE OF tender PARENTAL AFFECTION.

These things being so, blessed be God's gracious name, it is plain what he means (1 Cor. vii., 14), where he says such as soon as born ARE HOLY, and others are the opposite: even as he explains it himself of the children of Israel who were so situated and favoured, namely, "Thou ART an holy people unto the Lord . . . . that thou MAYEST BE an holy people unto the Lord thy God." 'Thou art by me made from the womb the subject of a godly parent's prayers and cares, which I hear and regard; that in my time of merciful visitation, in answer to, and by means of these, I may pour my spirit and blessing upon thee, and make thee holy unto myself by the circumcision of thine heart and renewal of thy spirit, to know, love, and serve me like my servant thy parent; and this will I do for mine own name's sake in thy salvation, and as a reward (of grace) to thy mother that bare thee, or thy father who begat thee, or both of them.' Another thing seems plain also, the REASON WHY a believer's family are to be

BAPTIZED ON ACCOUNT OF HIS FAITH;

even to bring out to view and impress the truth precious

to such parents that THEY have special reason for expecting the "blessing." WHEN the parent becomes a believer in Jesus, immediately, THROUGH HIS FAITH, the position of all his children becomes most favorably altered from what it was in his unbelief; for he receives from that moment a new parental heart, which flows out to them and God for them, and brings them under influences in private, in the family, and in the church (Rom. iii., 1, 2), all of a most precious nature. That being so, THEIR being *baptized* on account of HIS being a *believer* is seen to harmonize with their divinely favoured condition from the same reason, which condition they occupy simply as children of his of any age, while grace may be expected to be given them to believe also, in God's own time and way.

Yet, as we have observed before, the Lord has not PROMISED to make all the children of his people believers,—to save them all. To believe that would be a very dangerous error in its operation. The carnal Jews in our Saviour's time seem to have been under it. (Matt. iii.) Hence I remark next the EXTENT of fulfilment of this Covenant Promise appears to be

IN PROPORTION TO THE PARENT'S FAITHFULNESS.

"The soul of the sluggard desireth and hath nothing; but the soul of the diligent shall be made fat." This principle operates in divine things, as in worldly. "The effectual fervent prayer of a RIGHTEOUS man availeth *much*." Which means that the more grace we have, and the more we are truly devoted to the Lord's service in every way, the greater will be our influence with him in prayer, and the more will He bless our labours to others. "*According to* your faith be it unto you," indicates the same. Absalom died in his sins, no doubt, and for his own wickedness; yet we see that the sins of his father David in the matter of Uriah the Hittite were also at the bottom of the occasion of it. (2 Sam. xii. 11, 12; xvi. 20, 21; xviii. 14.) Eli's sons died for their own wickedness; yet Eli's unfaithfulness was God's reason for doing it. (1 Sam. iv. 11, 18; ii. 34, 29.) Every one who believes in Christ is an heir of the inheritance of the saints in light, and will be saved himself and herself. Yet there are great differences in degrees of grace among believers. Some have much higher attainments in knowledge, righteousness, and true holiness than others. Some are much more devoted, have more faith, love, humility, and obedience. Besides salvation to self, God adds many blessings in this life to, and by means of his people, in proportion to their devotion to him and his will according to the talents and opportunities they have received. The salvation of their offspring is one of these, for which, besides a careful, faithful, personal walk with God, means have to be diligently employed for them. The prize is great, and to be attained must be proportionately sought after. The more a parent is thus devoted in duty, the more full may he or she expect the promise fulfilled, "I will pour My spirit on thy seed, and My blessing on thine offspring. One shall say, I am the Lord's; and *another* shall call himself by the name of Jacob ; and ANOTHER shall subscribe with his hand to the Lord, and surname himself by the name of Israel." And so on till it may be, and sometimes is, that ALL the family, even in the parents' lifetime, are seen with themselves the children of the living God, in the highest sense, and adorning the doctrine of God our Saviour, *their* lips also a well of life, and many arising and calling them blessed. (Prov. x. 11; xxx. 28.) This is the bright and beautiful side. But there is another side as well. We believe that under God more depends on parents for the future well-being of their children in connection with salvation than upon any others in the world. We see it is so in temporal things. Ah, the responsibility is very great, even as much as the momentous interests are! The "church" of the living God has its great value and its place, yet the parents' is on the whole greater. When they fill it, it will include the various means and influences of Zion, and the divine manifestations there, and the others that belong to the daily home besides.

How sad that any parents, with all their tender natural affections, should yet be found with love so limited as not to heed though their precious charge should spend eternity in hell, and similarly of themselves! But O, sadder still, if any believers should be content with the hope of their own salvation, but so weak in love and heedless as not to seek diligently their family's, up to the last hour, as much, and more also, than they are awake and forward to labour on and suffer much throughout the years for their worldly well-being! If there be any of you, brethren and sisters, in a too careless condition, let me beseech you by the mercies and fear of the Lord, by His vows that are upon you, and by the value of the precious souls of your offspring, to rouse up again, lay hold on God according to His "exceeding great and precious promises," and seek their life with all earnestness and faith. They are in iminent peril if not yet believers. The promise is not, as you are aware, "I will be a God unto thee and to *all* thy seed after thee." The largeness or smallness of the number will depend, under him, chiefly ON YOU, just as the number converted in any particular place depends—as the rule—on the faith, love, diligence, and prayerfulness of Christian labourers. If any of your children perish, they will perish, no doubt, for their sins, but God could give grace to awaken, convert, and save. Let them not be left unvisited by him on account of your not wrestling with him to undertake for them—to reveal Christ in them the hope of glory, and your not instructing them sufficiently in the knowledge of Him.

As to our doctrine that FAITH can be Scripturally exercised IN BEHALF OF OTHERS, as is done in the baptism of our children, there ought to be no difficulty by any who accept the New and Old Testaments as God's Word. It certainly is a Scripture doctrine, and a very precious one; which should not be denied, ridiculed, or clouded for sectarian objects, but held high up to view, and proclaimed as from the housetops. The miracles the Saviour wrought on earth in proof of his Messiahship were exhibitions not only of his Almightiness, and the merciful nature of his mission, but also illustrations of his spiritual blessings, and the principles on which he proceeds in their conveyance. Now we see, as he teaches in regard to the highest blessings—"And him that cometh to me I will in no wise cast out," that not only did he not reject or send empty away ANY who came to him for cures to *themselves*, but also cured absent (or present) sons and daughters, servants and neighbours, on the petition of parents, masters, and friends, and ON ACCOUNT OF FAITH, not of the cured, but OF THE PETITIONERS: as, for examples, the centurion's servant (Matt. viii. 6, 11, 13); the woman of Canaan's daughter (chap. xv. 22, 28); the daughter of the ruler, Jairus (Mark v. 22, 36, 41). The Scripture also draws our attention in very particular terms to the man sick of the palsy, who was let down before Jesus by his four friends through the roof. (Mark ii. 5; Matt. ix. 2.) Of this it is said, "WHEN Jesus saw THEIR faith, he said unto the sick of the palsy, Son, THY SINS be FORGIVEN thee." Thereafter he also cured him of his bodily ailment. But it is most surely believed by all Christians that God answers the prayers and labours of "faith that worketh by love" of his people, in behalf of those, who, for the time, and for some time to come, may be altogether prayerless and godless themselves; and that the exercise of faith towards God in Christ in relation to others than ourselves, believers AND UNBELIEVERS, in acts of that nature, is a divinely warranted, nay, a graciously commanded thing, with broad grounds, and exceedingly great and precious promises. And that is what is done in baptizing, and in praying for and instructing children in the word of God, when we use those ordinances aright. It is that Jesus may cure and save them by his own supernatural power and grace—by baptizing them with the Holy Ghost sent down from heaven.

I have now, brethren, brought my undertaking on this subject to a close, though I have far from exhausted it. I have only been clearing it round and fencing it from the aims of misguided assailants, in which we have but touched by the way the valuable truths it is based upon, and in a lively though simple manner represents and seals with divine assurance. As when we observe the bow in the clouds we see the heaven appointed seal of the divine promise that he will not again destroy the earth with a flood; so in the baptism of our children the believer is to see a God appointed sign and seal of his gracious promise, "I will be a God unto thee, and to thy seed after thee;" "I will pour my spirit upon thy seed, and my blessing on thine offspring." And in faith and joy to sing—

> O Lord my God full many are
> The wonders thou hast done;
> Thy gracious thoughts to usward far
> Above all thoughts are gone.

> For unto them that do him fear
>   God's mercy never ends;
> And to their children's children still
>   His righteousness extends.
>
> The children of thy servants shall
>   Continually endure;
> And in thy sight, O Lord, their seed
>   Shall be established sure.
>
> That nation blessed is, whose God
>   JEHOVAH is, and those
> A blessed people are, whom for
>   His heritage he chose!

Although my subject at first on Infant baptism was the early church history of it, I have given you in addition some specimens of what we find on it in Scripture; and from all that has been set before you, my brethren, you may certainly see it is no relic of popery, but a precious RELIC OF THE APOSTLES and the WORD and WILL OF GOD.

THE MODE OF ADMINISTERING BAPTISM

you will understand, is quite a different question from that we have been considering, viz., the *persons to be* baptized. On that subject I have not space or leisure to enter at length, but will make some remarks. All familiar with the spoken and printed statements of Baptists will be aware that they often affirm that *the majority of learned Infant baptist writers* admit that the Greek word *baptizo* properly signifies "to dip or immerse," after their immersion theory. But on this let me quote you from their modern leader, Dr. Carson, in his learned work "On Baptism," now before me,—Edition, 1860. A "lexicographer," let me explain, is one who writes a dictionary of a language. When not aware or sure of the proper meaning of any word we look for it in such a book; and it is by dictionaries—or lexicons as they are called—of other languages that we are enabled to learn and know them. Keeping this in mind, hear Dr. Carson. He says (p. 55), "My position is that *baptizo* always signifies to dip, never expressing anything but *mode*. Now, as I have ALL THE LEXICOGRAPHERS and COMMENTATORS against me in this opinion," etc. Out of many I will give you one or two illustrations of how this idea, ' to dip, always to dip, and only to dip,' is applied. The Apostle states (1 Cor. x. 2) of the Israelites in their Exodus from Egypt that " they were all *baptized* unto Moses in the cloud and in the sea." Of this great event we have a particular account in Exodus xiv. 15–31; from which we learn that " the pillar of the cloud," in which was " Jehovah," went from before their face and stood behind them (ver. 19, 24), and they walked across the sea bottom on dry ground. We all know what dipping a person into the sea is, and see from the narrative they WERE NOT DIPPED at all in it—nor in the cloud. Still Paul says they WERE *baptized* in them. There was there, therefore, what the Holy Spirit and Paul regard as baptism where there was no dipping. But let us hear Carson on it. He says, " the baptism of the Israelites in the Red Sea was a DRY baptism ; " " Moses *walked* on dry ground. Yes, and he got a DRY DIP." (Carson on baptism, p. 120, 329, 413). According to that definition of *baptizo* as always and only to *dip*, Baptists contend that it should be so translated in Scripture wherever it occurs. Well, let us try it with a few specimens as they wish,—" I indeed dip you in water unto repentance ; but he (Jesus) will dip you *in the Holy Ghost and fire*." " Ye shall be dipped *in the Holy Ghost* not many days hence." " Know ye not that as many of us as were dipped *into Jesus Christ* were dipped *into his death*." " For by one Spirit are we all dipped *into one body*." (Mat. iii. 11 ; Acts i. 5 ; Rom. vi. 3 ; 1 Cor. xii. 13). To serious minds in general I think this will appear no improvement in these passages, but from the nature of the connections, awfully improper! In the Baptist New Testament, now before me, (Edition 1873), the translation is as above, except that it has the word *immerse* for dip, which, however, they contend has precisely the same meaning. Well, *dip* is a clear English Saxon word, while *immerse*, which is wholly from the Latin, is more obscure, and, unlike the other, does not imply a taking out again (nor is that the only difference). A stone cast into the sea is *immersed* though it remain at the bottom ever after. You would not say it was *dipped*. It is noteworthy, however, that while in all their books, etc., they contend that *dip* and *immerse* have just one and the same meaning, that Version has never once translated *baptize* and its derivatives by *dip*, but always by *immerse*,—the more obscure term, although it and its cognates *baptized, baptizing, baptism*, occur in the New Testament upwards of a hundred times. Strange that they never once rendered it by *dip*. It is also remarkable that that Version which was prepared especially to carry out the Baptist contention of translating *baptizo* and its different forms by *their* one meaning only, has not been found acceptable to the great majority of Baptists. On this it is significant that about a year ago, on my sending for a copy of it to the Baptist Book Room, Toronto, I received reply that there was not one in stock, and I had to send for it to Philadelphia, U.S.! Besides, the fact of its existence is kept so quiet that few people know there is such a Version. They don't use it in their churches, and very little anywhere so far can be seen. In the *Canadian Baptist* of 28th Oct. last, is an article on it, which regretfully admits its general disfavour among them, and says, "It has a handy place in many libraries, and it is much consulted, but *very few congregations* hear it read." "A good many of us while immersing believers on the profession of their faith, will still call the act a *baptism*, and insist that nothing else is entitled to the name." Yet (by the way) the Baptists of Britain and America would not co-operate with the British and Foreign Bible Society, and the American one because these societies refused to give their funds for the issue of New Testaments, having that word translated always by *dip*. (Carson, p. 378, Cramp's Catech. p. 51.) Now, when their own version was issued, one would suppose they would all favour, procure, praise, and use it universally in preference to ours, since they maintain as beyond question that baptizo means dipping only, and that much dishonesty and injury has been done by ours not having it so translated. Well, they did favour the idea of its publication at first, and were eager to get a copy, but on perusal felt inclined to keep it in obscurity. And why? Does it not clearly render *baptize* everywhere by immerse—a thing they had longed for and feel so important? Yes, but strange things appeared also with it. Then appeared such expressions as "*dipped* in the Holy Spirit," *dipped* into Christ," "*dipped* into his death," and a number of others, which, explained as they may be, impress the inward feeling and conviction that something must be seriously wrong that shocks the mind. I don't wonder that they don't find inclination to read that Version in public, and such like portions, and that they make no efforts to circulate it as they do other books. Also by keeping it out of stock in their Book Rooms and saying as little as possible about it, their own people who have not seen it, and others outside, will necessarily not find or see it.

The other word BAPTO (the root word from which *baptizo* is derived) they also used to contend, *always* signified " to *dip* or *immerse*," till about forty years ago, when Dr. Carson's work was published. In that work is a number of passages from ancient Greek writers in which *bapto* appears. The following is one (p. 48):—" The LAKE WAS BAPTED in the blood of a mouse." Baptists used to render this—" The *lake* was *dipped* in the blood of a mouse," and said it was a figure of poetry. On this, however, Dr. Carson remarks—" What a monstrous paradox in rhetoric is the figuring of the *dipping* of a lake in the blood of a mouse! Yet Dr. Gale [an eminent Baptist writer] supposes the lake dipped by hyperbole. 'The literal sense,' he says, ' is the lake was dipped in blood.' Never was there such a figure. The lake is not said to be *dipped* in blood, but to be dyed with blood." He adds, " There is in the word (here) no reference to *mode*. Had Baptists entrenched themselves here, they would have saved themselves much useless toil, and much false criticism, without straining to the impeachment of their candour or their taste."

This censure of his brethren was really merited by them and still is in many things ; yet Dr. Carson renders himself subject to the same, as fully as he gave it. He saw the Baptists' main objects were not advanced by insisting that *bapto* always meant to dip. He therefore resolved to concede to us that in *a certain class* of operations it often has not that signification at all, viz.: when connected with colouring of any kind. But when the connection is water, or when the object is not to colour, he maintains it only and always means to *dip*. To yield the point outside of colouring would be equivalent to giving up the whole contention, on account of the connection of *baptizo* as the derivative of *bapto*. In pages 44-48, he quotes a number of the passages we present against the dipping theory, of which, besides the one about the lake and the blood of a mouse, just mentioned, the following are one or two more specimens, viz.: "When the colouring liquid DROPS UPON the garments they are *bapted*" (stained.) "Nearchus relates that the Indians *bapt* (dye) their beards." "The old man endeavoured to conceal the hoariness of his hair by *bapting* (dyeing) it." "The lady's yellow locks were not *bapted* (coloured) by *art*, but by *nature*," etc. On these and others Carson says, (p. 46), "Bapto signifies to dye *by sprinkling* as properly as by *dipping*, though originally it was by the latter. Nor is he (Dr. Gale, Baptist), well founded when he asserts that the word in such applications always implies and refers to its primary signification only. On the contrary, I have produced some examples, *and he himself has produced others*, in which candour cannot say there is any such implication or reference. From such examples it could not be known even that *bapto* has the meaning of *dip*. They relate to *dyeing* wholly without any reference to *dipping*; nay, some of them with an expressed reference to another mode." Now observe here Carson's REASON for admitting *bapto* in such instances to be used without reference to dipping, and with reference to sprinkling and the like as the mode, *is because* this is seen by the nature of the cases themselves, or from what is stated of the mode of *bapto* in them. Candour, he concedes, requires this admission on such evidence; on which we only wonder it could be denied by the other Baptist writers for centuries. But we also contend equally that WHEREVER the word appears to be used similarly, though not connected with colouring at all, he and those who follow him are bound in consistency to admit the same; that if a person or thing is said to be *bapted* by sprinkling clean water, for example, and not by dipping, then candour requires that it does not mean dipping there, but relates to sprinkling. It would follow, however, if the latter were proven, that the word *bapto* in connection with liquid of any kind, would mean *wetting* without reference to any mode in particular as the only one. But on this Carson also, to use his own expression, expends "much false criticism, with straining to the impeachment of his candour and his taste." I will give you one specimen of his reasoning in this connection.

The example I will refer to is in Daniel (chap. iv. 33; v. 21), where it is stated in historical narrative of Nebuchadnezzar that "he was driven from men, and did eat grass as oxen, and his body was WET WITH THE DEW OF HEAVEN." In the Septuagint Greek Translation of the Old Testament, the expression in both passages is, "And his body was BAPTED with the dew of heaven." Now, here is a decidedly clear case in nature and mode; nor is the idea of dyeing involved. Nor, looking at the passages before and after, does it appear that Daniel refers to the greatness of the dew, but simply to the fact, that among the other things in which the king of Babylon's condition was reduced to that of beasts, he had not the shelter of a human habitation, but was under the open canopy of heaven, exposed to the dews of night, whether little or great, "till seven times (years) passed over him." Moreover, never did DEW fall to such extent in quantity that a man could be "dipped" in it. For that it would require to accumulate several feet deep on the ground. To shew its profuseness in some countries, Carson (p. 85) quotes from Dr. Gale (Baptist) as follows :—" That incomparable mathematician, Captain Halley, observed, when making some experiments in St. Helena, that the dews fell in such abundance as to make HIS PAPER too wet to WRITE on, and his glasses unfit for use without frequent wiping." Well, granting all that, could a man be "dipped" in what would only make paper too wet to write on? Dr. Gale could not venture to affirm this. Carson (p. 86) says :—" Dr. Gale absurdly supposes that *bapto* means to cover with water, *without reference to mode,* and at the same time metaphorically alludes to *dipping*. Neither Daniel nor his translators say, that Nebuchadnezzar should be as wet *as if* he were dipped; for if that had been the expression, there could have been no dispute about it." Carson next differs similarly from Dr. Cox, (Baptist), whom he quotes as saying: —" It has been generally replied [by Baptists] that a body exposed to eastern dews would be *as* wet *as if* plunged into water;" "it does *not* imply *the mode* by which the body of the king was wetted, but its *condition* as *resulting from* exposure to the dew of heaven." To this Dr. Carson replies :—" Without doubt the verb EXPRESSES *mode* here as well as anywhere else. To suppose the contrary gives up the point at issue, as far as the mode is concerned. This, in fact, makes *bapto* signify simply to *wet*, without reference to mode." His own decision is (p. 35), "The words of the Septuagint are, ' his body was IMMERSED in the dew.'" He thereupon characterizes as " a SOULLESS critic," unable to appreciate the "beauties of poetry," any who objects against this rendering, that " there was here no literal immersion," or dipping. Drs. Gale and Cox would be among those "soulless" critics, though doubtless not behind in zeal as Baptists. Again (p. 38), he says:—"The man exposed to a SUMMER PLUMP will say that he has got a complete *dipping*. This is the very expression of Daniel. One mode of wetting is FIGURED as ANOTHER mode of wetting *by the liveliness of* the imagination." 1. He here compares the very gentle fall of dew, such as after awhile would make "paper too wet to write on," to a heavy torrent of rain!—no doubt from the liveliness of his imagination, not from sober reasoning. 2. I have never yet heard any exposed even to a heavy plump of *rain* say they had got "a complete *dipping*," but rather that they had got a complete *dripping*, which is somewhat like the other word in sound, but quite different in meaning, and suits drenching from a *down-pour*.

In this example, brethren, is seen a clear case of *bapto* wetting by *sprinkling on* the person, just as distincly as those other cases Dr. C. acknowledged had no reference to dipping because the *bapting* in them was seen to have been by a different mode. Hence we reason thus, If (to use his own expression) "candour cannot say in those examples that there is any implication or reference to dipping, but to sprinkling" and the like, he therefore admits it to be *absurd* to say it *has* a reference to dipping there; for the same reason it is equally absurd to maintain *here* that the inspired historian affirms that Nebuchadnezzar's body was *dipped in* the dew, when manifestly he was not, but that he was sprinkled with it. A cause whose ablest advocates feel constrained for its maintenance to resist the application of this self-evidently just principle of interpretation in this and similar cases, and that, too, while its justice is (though tardily) admitted in others, is self-condemned and consciously cannot stand the test of ever consistent truth.

One feature particularly seen all through Dr. Carson's

work, is his strong, unhesitating affirmations ; in which also he makes many contradictory statements, the pointing out of which would occupy many pages. For instance, on *baptizo*, (p. 61), he give this sentence from a Greek writer, " Thou mayest be *baptized*, O bladder ; but thou art not fated to sink ;" in which baptizing seems not to admit of *sinking*. He explains, however, that the word for " to sink," here, " is characteristically applied to things that *sink of themselves* to the bottom," that is, *by their own weight*. According to this, then, what is *baptizable* would be, " what will *not* sink of its own weight," such as a bladder. Yet on another case he seeks to explain he says (p. 284), a thing " is said to be UN*baptizable* because it will *not* dip or sink *by its own weight*." This seems a contradiction *in terms* of his explanation of the former. Again, in the statement about the Pharisees in Mark vii. 4, " Except they wash they eat not ;" the word for wash is *baptizo*. On this Dr. C. remarks (p. 68), " It ought to have been translated, ' except they *dip themselves* they eat not.'" But on another case (p. 30), he says, " The person dips *himself, therefore* it is *bapto* to dip, *and* NOT *baptizo*, to cause to dip." I have before quoted you his statement (p. 55, 67, etc.) " My position is that *baptizo always* signifies to dip, *never* expressing anything but MODE." According to this the word baptism is just dipping, nothing more nor less, and a *real* baptism can only be where there is really a dipping. Yet on Acts ii. 2-3 (p. 107), he says, " As respects the transaction on the day of Pentecost there was a REAL baptism ;" " the disciples were literally COVERED with the *appearance* of wind and fire ;" " were completely covered with the emblems of the spirit." He calls it a " real baptism " since it is so named by God's word; but was it a dipping withal ? He admits " they were not dipped," but really *baptized* (a word that he says never means *anything* but dip) *by* being *covered* without dipping. Yet again, afterwards, (p. 267) in reply to an opponent's definition of a meaning of *baptizo*, he answers firmly, " There is neither COVERING nor water in the word." Also (p. 479) " *No* person *is* baptized who is not immersed" (dipped.) And (p. 36) " If all the water in the ocean had *fallen on* him, it would not have been a litteral immersion "—that is, a baptism or dipping. Hence, after all, the *covering* of the disciples was not a baptism at all, since that is not its meaning, nor were they *dipped* into "the *sound* of a rushing mighty wind," nor into the "cloven tongues like as of fire which *sat* on each of them." But God in his word says they were really baptized then. *His* baptism, therefore, and Carson's are not the same in mode.

The inconsistent method of interpretation which Carson adopts with *bapto* he also applies to *baptizo*, and then, over and again, to meet difficulties, replies that he has *established* that it means throughout the history of the language, only and always to dip, and that, though in many of the instances he refers to there is confessedly no dipping, nor possibility of it.

In page 21 he quotes Dr. Gale, who is reasoning from an instance in which the sea coast is said to be baptized by the tide flowing *over* it, as follows :—"The word *baptizo* perhaps does not so necessarily express the action of putting under water, as in general a thing being in that condition, *no matter how* it comes so, whether it is put into the water, or the water comes over it." To this he replies, "In any particular instance when *this word* is applied to an object lying under water, but NOT actually DIPPED, the mode essentially denoted by it IS AS TRULY EXPRESSED as in any other instance of its occurrence. Indeed the *whole beauty* of such expressions consists in the expression of a mode NOT REALLY belonging to the thing expressed." Such is the principle on which he proves his one meaning, which Drs. Gale, Cox, Fuller, Morell, etc., all in the front rank of Baptist scholars, were too dull to perceive the beauty of, though willing enough. Thus also on the baptism of the 3,000 on Pentecost, he says (p. 354), "I will not suffer my opponents to call on me to guage the fountains and ponds that were in Jerusalem eighteen centuries back. Whether they used baths or cisterns is quite alike to me. They *must* have been immersed, for the word has no other meaning." Again, on Mark vii. 4, where he admits the "tables" there ought to have been translated couches or beds, he says (p. 451), "The couches were immersed, (dipped), because the word which is employed to express the operation has this signification, and no other."

Our position, on the other hand, is that *baptizo*, like *bapto*, is not confined in its history to one mode, but like the expressions, to wet, to burn, scald, tinge, or dye, wash, cleanse, bathe, etc., etc., is fulfilled by various modes of action. Each of these things can be done by dipping, but in other ways as well. The last mentioned—*bathe*, Baptists usually affirm to be equivalent to dip. Hence Carson remarks (p. 326-7), " If bathing was required does not this imply immersion ? " " Bathings were appointed by God, and bathings imply immersion." Well, it is a very common operation to bathe the brow, or a wound in the head, the arm, or the body. Do we never bathe these except by dipping them ? We bathe ourselves by dipping and swimming ; can we not vary it by a shower bath ?—a very common thing in cities. Is that a shower dipping ? And, like myself, brethren, you have no doubt bathed your whole body in a tub in your room with small depth of water, lifting it up on your body. Hence the divine appointment would be fulfilled by the latter mode, etc., as properly as by any other. Among the other kinds of misrepresentation to which Baptists are addicted, they adopt a distinctly

GROSS FALLACY ON THE ACTUAL MEANING OF WORDS.

Dr. Cramp, in reference to all language, states it thus: (Catechism on Baptism p. 33) " *Every word* has *one* natural, obvious, original meaning *which will be applied to it by all* readers or hearers and with which it will be used by speakers and writers. From that natural and primary meaning other senses, acceptations or uses may branch out, but they *will* imply or include the ORIGINAL idea." This is stated, not as an opinion, but an indubitable fact, and coming from a learned professor of a Baptist College, it will be the more readily accepted as true by the Baptist community; besides it is one of their main positions. Yet nothing could be more contrary to the actual truth than the above statement, nor does it require much acquaintance with words to know this.

You will observe, brethren, the above is affirmed of " EVERY WORD." Now *bapto* is admitted to be a primary word, and although they contend for its original meaning as to *dip*, yet I have shown you examples in Carson where that meaning is *not* included in it, and that himself acknowledged (p. 133) that "from them it could not be known even that it has that meaning" at all. But let us look at some words of our own language by which all of you will see easily for yourselves. Take 1. Cunning. When our English Bible was translated 250 years ago, its common meaning was "honest skill," (Exod. xxvi. 1; xxxi. 3, 4), but now it *always* means *deceit*. What resemblance will "all readers," etc., see between these? 2. Craft. Paul (Acts xviii. 3) was "by craft, a tentmaker," and still it is used for an "honest trade;" it also signifies *deceit*. 3. Wife. This, like most of the words of our language, is of Anglo-Saxon (German) origin, is from the verb *weben*, to weave, and originally meant a *weaver*. In primitive times the weaving was done at home by the married women while the unmarried daughters *spun* the yarn. Hence the married woman or mother came to be called the weaver,—wife. It is now used as the universal term for *married* woman, without reference at all to its original meaning, which very few even know. 4. Spinster, for the reason just stated, was the name given an unmarried daughter—that is, a spinner. In my marriage registration papers one of the printed questions I have to answer is, Was the bride a spinster or a widow? the former of which terms means now simply an unmarried woman, and in law is applied to all in that condition from the hamlet to the palace. That is, the present use of the word in that connection is not its original meaning at all. 5. Villain, was at first pronounced in three syllables, vill-a-en, and signified (1) a serf attached to the villa (the name then of the country house) of a baron of early times. (2) After the abolition of serfdom, any country peasant. (3) One of the working people in city or country. (4) Now, only a scoundrel. This last refers only to a bad moral character of any rank in society; while the first three meanings had no bearing on the moral character. The last does not convey to us in its use anything about serfdom, a baron, or his villa. Neither did the second or third. 6. Prevent,—is made up of two Latin words, *vent*, to come, and *pre*, before; which combined were its first meaning. Thus, "In the morning shall my prayer prevent (come before) thee." "Mine eyes prevent the night watches" (Ps. lxxxviii. 13; cxix. 147-8). But now its meaning is quite different—*to hinder*. 7. Let—to *hinder* (Rom. i. 13; 2 Thes. ii. 7), and also to *permit*. 8. Passion —simply *suffering* (Acts i. 3); (2) longing desire; (3) violent anger. 9. Fast—to walk fast (quickly); to tie fast (securely). The tying may be done ever so slowly, while in the former case "fast" means *speed* of motion. To these add, to fast (abstain), a fast (loose living) man. Each of these are from the same original word. I might go on thus filling page after page, many words being completely, and others much altered in signification, and many with radically different meanings in use at the same periods past and present. Thus, body—of man,—of men (organized association),—of water; also civil, charity, bachelor, church, hell, offend, carriage, grace, conversation, etc. In these respects all languages have the same history, being mutable like all other human things. Dr. Cramp's and the Baptist doctrine that the first or *original* meaning of every word of a language is in its use always applied—that is, meant to be conveyed,—and is understood by all writers, readers, and hearers in every age, is remarkable, and, I have just shown you, very far from corresponding with the facts, and requires but a small amount of education and observation to see this. Yet although this has often been exhibited, the same thing continues printed and taught year after year, all to make the people they have access to believe that baptism must mean a dipping! You will observe that the range of words of the Greek LANGUAGE is not of any one age merely, but comprehends all the known writings of antiquity, from a thousand years before the Christian era, in all the different countries where it was spoken; during which there were no printed books and very little education among the myriads, with interminglings, alterations and modifications of peoples, languages, ideas, words, dialects of pronunciation, and things in general, going on even more than during the last thousand years in our own isolated sea girt English-speaking fatherland. After all it is the mass of the people which moulds the usage of words for themselves and succeeding posterity, and who from lack of education and other general and local causes, are not very particular or philosophic about the exact etymological or learned fitness of the words they use to express their ideas; and writers, etc., will use the words to express their ideas used for those ideas by those to whom they address themselves. Let me mention an illustration.

In my native Scotland, its hills are numerous, and some ascend very high, literally piercing through the clouds (when there are any lowering), often a considerable distance. To the highest only do they apply the term "mountain." When I came to Canada a few years ago, I was informed that there was a "mountain" at the back of the city of Hamilton. I expected a *great* elevation; but when I saw it, alas, it was just a "brae,"—the word in Scotland for one of the smallest of elevations. Were the people in Scotland to read in a Canadian newspaper of "the mountain" at Hamilton, they would certainly fancy an elevation with a peak about touching the sky! The reason for the difference of application of the term here no doubt is local, from the few and small elevations in our Province. Another recent modification is the colonial word "bush." This word was formerly applied to something very small, as a rose or currant bush, or a small branch of a tree with a decent share of leaves; but never was thought to be at all equal to a *tree*, which was a giant in comparison. But our Canadian and other colonists have disregarded that old fashioned idea, and, as if a *forest* of *trees* a hundred miles square, more or less, were a little thing, have got into the habit of calling that a *bush*, and newspapers, book writers, and ministers, etc., when they refer to it, feel they must call it a "bush" to be at once understood. A piece of wood for holding a candle gave the name at first to Candle*stick*; but though made of brass it is still called by the same name. To *Macadamize* a road, is used in Scotland, some parts of Canada, etc., after the inventor's name, for overlaying it with "metal," as it is called. By and by, if people take the notion, it may be used for the changing of a young woman's name into "Mrs. Macadam;" and might afterwards, if that happened to please the popular fancy, become the term commonly used for marriages in general. On the same principle we see surnames of persons applied. The expression, "covering a road with *metal*," in the connection just mentioned, would be thought by people in the past and by many still, to mean—with *iron*, or gold and silver if you please; but the real sense in which it is used would not be imagined, namely, with coarsely broken, smallish, hard (whin) *stones*.

Such brethren is the process of genuine fact in this subject; the real philosophy of the actual meaning of words. And it is with *facts* we have to do. The word of God was given in the language of the common people of the various periods when its books were written, an entirely new meaning or application being attached to a few words, which it fully explains, as 'life,' 'death,' 'spiritual,' in the gospel senses, and 'supper' as applied to the participation of a very small portion of the bread and sip of the wine of the second emblematical ordinance of the Christian church, while the term always signified and signifies a full meal in other connections.

There is just one other point I will advert to. Baptists are in the habit of quoting from Infant baptist writers, etc., that *baptizo*, in the Greek LANGUAGE, signifies *to immerse*, without stating the other meanings also given, and from that as an admission of this as the ONLY proper meaning, accuse those writers of inconsistent practice, and insist that it ought always to be so translated in Scripture. Of this we had a recent instance in the Baptist church here. Rev. Mr. Carnes, in one of a series of discourses on Baptism, related, on the reported authority of Professor Angus, of the Baptist College, London, Eng., that the Committee of theologians of different denominations (of which Dr. A. is one) at present revising the New Testament, *unanimously* admitted that the word *baptizo* signified (in the Greek language) "TO IMMERSE," yet refused so to translate it in their edition of the New Testament. When this latter sentence was concluded by Mr. Carnes (in a tone of indignation) the Baptists near him cried out "Shame! shame!" which (all the more that it was Sabbath evening) indicated strong censure of the Committee. On the following Thursday evening, at the beginning of my lecture on Baptism (reproduced at the beginning of this treatise), I repeated what Mr. Carnes had said, as now related, and asked him (who was present) to correct me in anything I had not stated correctly. He rose to say he had not said that Dr. Angus had informed him, for he had it from another to whom Dr. A. had told it. I requested him if there was any other part not correctly reported to say so. He made no further correction. I then said, "Though that account is given as hearsay we will suppose it correct. That

Committee then unanimously admitted *baptizo* to signify *immerse*. And I add that I freely admit *the same*. But don't mistake me. In saying that I don't mean that it ALWAYS signifies to immerse, for I believe it does not, from my own examination of its usage, in the Greek language, and that is just the point. The Committee were not reported by Mr. Carnes to have said that. Nor did he state their reason for refusing to translate the word by *immerse*, wherever it occurs in the New Testament. I have no doubt their reason was that while it often is used of immersion in the Greek language they were well aware that it often did not mean that; and were therefore to be commended for refusing to translate it by that word on the ground that it always signifies it when it often does not. Suppose, *e.g.*, the English word "craft." You and I will unanimously admit that that word does really signify *deceit* in our language. But if on the ground of that acknowledgment I am requested to translate it wherever I find it by the word *deceit* I cannot but refuse. And why? Because while that is its meaning often, it often is not, both in Scripture and out of it. It also means an honest 'manual trade,' such as Paul's, Aquila's, and Priscilla's, of whom we are told in the Acts (xviii. 3), they were "of the same *craft*," namely, "tent makers;" that is, "by *craft* they were tent makers." How would it do to translate that expression by "by *deceit* they were tent makers?" There are hundreds of other words in our language that have more than one meaning in their usage. *Baptizo* is similar in the Greek language. If we had been told the Revisal Committee's reason for refusing to render it always by *immerse*, as Baptists wish, there would have been no room to cry Shame! Shame! against them, as was done on Sabbath evening in the Baptist church, who only acted as reasonable men.

On this again let me quote you a statement of Pengilly (Scrip. guide to Bap., p. 13, note at bottom) on the meaning of *baptizo*, as "to dip or plunge," he says, "We might call to our assistance lexicographers and other learned writers out of number; but I may with confidence affirm that in citing *one*, we cite *every* competent authority on the subject; for in THE *proper* and primary sense of the word *baptize*, learned men of all classes and countries are agreed, as I shall show in the Appendix." Along side of this let me now give you again the statement on this of his cotemporary Dr. Carson, whose work on Baptism was first published only some two or three years after Pengilly's. He says (p. 55;) " My position is, that *baptizo* always signifies to dip; never expressing anything but mode. Now, as I have ALL the lexicographers and commentators AGAINST ME in *this* opinion." etc. Now would any one reading and believing that in Pengilly, expect this from Carson, and is it likely the latter would weaken his cause by it if it were not very true? There is this also, Pengilly's book is a small one, circulated (by the Bapt. Pub. Soc.) among the common people, who know very little of lexicographers and commentators (learned writers) themselves; while Carson's is large, and meant more especially for others. Pengilly, at the close of his statement, promises to show its truth in the Appendix. In p. 71, he begins to give quotations for this purpose. After giving his second he refers the reader to a note at the bottom, as follows, " See this author (Calvin) and those that follow cited at greater length and their work referred to in Booth's *Pædobaptist Examined*. Vol. I., pp. 44 to 65. EIGHTY-TWO such authorities are there adduced." So it seems to take his quotations second hand from Booth. Nor are there many readers of Pengilly likely to be able to examine Booth, and after that to verify Booth again by looking up the books of the original authors, quoted in Booth. I find these remarks necessary of both Pengilly and Booth; as we have already seen, in numerous instances they were decidedly addicted to genuine deliberate misquotations, which I have shown you at length at the beginning. And besides those I have shown you from Booth, you will recollect of Rev. Peter Edwards, Baptist Minister, that he was led to leave the Baptist church by reading the same book of Booth's, from seeing the unfair manner in which he represented the writers he professed to quote, and on this Mr. Edwards make special mention in that way of *these same* "EIGHTY-TWO" writers Pengilly in his note refers to. (See p. 21.)

In these latter observations on the mode of administering the ordinance, as distinguished from the person to be baptized, I have sought to give you some insight into the process by which Baptists make out from the Greek language (which few of course are acquainted with) that its word for baptism was ever and only used to signify dipping. There are two quite different classes of Baptists (and have always been in their history) which ought to be distinguished by us the one from the other. The 'Open Communionists,' as that name indicates, take a different position in theory and practice on the importance of the subject from that of the 'Close Communionists.' They are disposed to hold communion at the Lord's table and otherwise with Christians of other denominations not baptized according to their views. This, however, the Close Communionists not only refuse to do, but in addition, will not even allow Open Communion Baptists that privilege with them, although baptized according to Baptist principles, because these don't regard the difference on that outward ceremonial ordinance so vital as to forbid their communing with their other fellow Christians. Mr. Spurgeon, for instance, for that reason they will not allow to sit at their communion table. They take pleasure in him as an illustrious Baptist minister, his sermons are constantly printed in their denominational weekly paper, the *Canadian Baptist*, etc. He is acknowledged to be *Christian* enough for the table—to commemorate the Lord's death, but he is not, in their esteem, *Baptist* enough. This feature of their position alone shows what very great importance they attach to the question of the baptism of water. In their denominational church property Title Deeds, for example (a copy of which I have before me), by which each of their congregations BINDS itself "to hold and maintain" a considerable number of specified doctrines, etc., is the following: "That Communion at the Lord's Table should be holden to those *only* who have been so immersed, *and who themselves thus practice*":—that is,—"and who themselves practice the holding of that Communion to those *only* who have been so immersed." This excludes all Open Communionists.

They justify their position thus: It is by baptism any is *admitted* into the visible church of Christ, after which is the Lord's table. But those not baptized according to their views are not baptized at all, and therefore not really admitted into, but still outside of the visible church, and should not in that position partake of the Lord's Supper or obtain the other privileges of members. According to this theory it follows that none in the world have been or are within the visible church of Christ, as members of it, but the Baptists alone. They alone have been and are his kingdom on earth. All our dispensations of the Lord's supper are therefore sacrileges. The great men of the Reformation, and before it, and since, that we have fondly looked upon as bright luminaries in and of the Lord's Zion, and the many many thousands of our infant baptist brethren throughout the lands and the ages who in genuine adoration of the blessed Saviour, assembled together for his worship, in caves or in churches, sat under and witnessed for his glorious evangel, and upheld his truth and honour amidst the fiercest persecutions, "bearing in their body the marks of the Lord Jesus," their limbs loaded with fetters, their blood spilled like rivers for his testimony and his name, or their bodies devoured by the burning flame—none, not one of these, according to that doctrine, did the Lord regard as members of his body the church, and entitled by him in "the breaking of bread" to express the faith in him they *had* and the love they *felt!* None of these would the Close Communion Baptists permit to sit with them at their Lord's table, nor sit down beside them at theirs! Also, besides those of more recent times, the multitude in the different denominations of shining lights, and of devoted Christian labourers at home and abroad, around us, in fatherlands and among the heathen, have no standing in *the* church,—not even as adherents of it, since they worship not in Baptist churches!

Well, there is ONE LUMINOUS FACT that must be admitted, which alone is significant enough to prove the erroneousness of this theory of baptism and close communionism, that may well console us and make up for the disacknowledgment of these Baptist brethren. It is this. The Lord Jesus himself, the head of the church, has acted and is acting quite otherwise. He has undoubtedly bestowed his salvation as extensively on Infant baptists, has poured out his spirit in as large measure on them, has carried on throughout the ages in every land, and advanced the interests of his spiritual kingdom, BY THEIR INSTRUMENTALITY, as much, and more also, by far, than he has among and by Close Communionists. And look around to-day. Is it only or preeminently among and by these latter he is doing his marvels of grace in Britain, Canada, the United States, Madagascar, the South Sea Islands, Italy, Spain, Mexico, etc., etc. ? They will not, they can not, answer in the affirmative. The preeminence is really on our side, though "not to us, not to us, but to his name be the glory." Moreover, any acquainted with the facts will have observed a considerable blight in these respects in that body as compared with the Open Communionists. They have great zeal for proselytism to their body, but genuine piety, a tender conscience in the matter of truth and the fear of the Lord, practical (that is real) love for the whole household of faith, and the winning of souls largely to Christ, appear much less their attainment.

This doctrine of theirs is of the same nature as the Romish and Puseyite one of Apostolic Succession. The advocates of the latter refuse to acknowledge to be in the church of Christ any of all dissenting ministers, ordinances and members, because not ordained, administered, and admitted in (according to them) the proper way—by the proper office-bearers. One satisfactory proof of their serious error is just such as we have been reviewing in the other case ; namely, that the Lord, the King of Zion, has undoubtedly blessed, and used as a means of blessing, those same dissenting ministers, people, and ordinances, and still does, as much as, nay much more (to say no more) than those of Rome or Puseyism. Now you will observe, brethren, that the regular Baptist Church, or Close Communionists, assume a similarly exclusive position, and the ground of that exclusiveness, though different as to the question, is of the same nature. In the one case it is the external. administration of baptism ; in the other, the external ordination of office-bearers. The upholders of the Apostolic Succession of Bishops, while very erroneous in that doctrine, yet in accordance with it, refuse to acknowledge the standing of dissenting *ministers* and people in what is held to belong only to those who are *in* the church. Hence, for example, they will not own that the former are ministers of the church, will not invite or allow them to officiate as such to *their* congregations, etc. This is consistent with their doctrine, but wrong in reality, because their doctrine is wrong in itself. In like manner, Close Communion Baptists, *if consistent*, would not acknowledge any Infant-baptist minister as a minister at all. For how can a man be a lawful minister, (that is to say, a minister at all) of the church of Christ, if he is not even a member of it—not to add, not even an adherent? The highest office with its very sacred duties, responsibilities, and influences, cannot surely be legitimately acknowledged where the very lowest standing of an ordinary member is not yet attained? If the ordinary membership be zealously guarded against the recognition of any not duly baptized, much more should the sacred ministry be guarded by the same parties by refusing to recognize, and by practically protesting against any as having that office who have not been so baptized, and who besides, according to the theory of baptism we are considering, teach and administer to others a false baptism and dispense the Lord's Supper to those who ought not to partake of it—they not having been immersed.

But the Close Communionists, whatever their motive be, don't carry out their doctrine to its obvious termination. This they shrink from. They do acknowledge the other denominations of the church; and speak of them *as such*, and the *ministers* of them, inviting them from time to time as ministers, officially, of the Christian Church to their tea meetings and to preach to them, etc., etc. Now there must be some strong reason to account for this short-coming; what can it be? Do they believe that in Christ's estimation none of these are ministers in and of HIS church? If they do why are they not declaring it as from the housetop (as decidedly and clearly as they insist that all, only sprinkled, are not members), and *as practically* refusing to acknowledge them throughout? It is only a short and is a necessary step in consistency from where they have halted. One advantage of this would be to awaken public attention, and enable people at large to perceive more fully and correctly the real import of their distinctive doctrine by what it necessarily leads to. Yet this is not done but the reverse is. The reason of which I presume is, something tells them that to take such a position merely on the question of water application, against ministers and denominations, who, in the great vital doctrines of Christianity, in Scripture piety, and in God in Christ evidently blessing them past and present, are at least as distinguished as themselves, would lead all reasonable people to conclude that their theory *must* be unscriptural like that of the Apostolical Succession; and would make the cause to which they have (unfortunately) committed themselves *altogether* unlikely to succeed.

I have in another place (Preface p. xvii.) given you the mind on this subject of the godly John Bunyan, and now will conclude with the sentiments of the illustrious Spurgeon, *Open* Communionist. Although we differ from him on the question of water baptism itself, that becomes a small matter when we see his proper understanding and spirit in giving it no more than its own subordinate place and value,—so different from that ascribed to it by Close Communionists. In the *Christian Guardian* (Methodist denominational weekly paper) of the 19th April, now before me, I find the following from " Spurgeon on Communion ;" in which he says,—" There is not a Christian beneath the scope of God's heaven from whom I am separated. At the Lord's table I always invite all Christians to come and sit down and commune with us. If any man were to tell me that I am separate from the Episcopalian, Presbyterian, or the Methodist, I would tell him he did not know me, for I love them with a pure heart fervently, and I am not separate from them." Then stating his esteem " for the strict-communion Baptists," he says of them, " They really do separate themselves from the great body of Christ's people. They say they will not commune with it ; and if any one come to their table who has not been baptized, they turn him away. The pulse of Christ is communion ; and woe to the church that seeks to cure the ills of Christ's Church by stopping its pulse ! "

This, brethren, is a worthy utterance of that Baptist minister and of the Church of Christ. It gives the question at issue its proper subordinate value and place. As to the rightness or wrongness of this or that mode and conditions of the administration of baptism it leaves freedom for enquiry by the proper means, but allows everyone to be fully persuaded in his own mind, with no bar to his communion with those he may differ from in that persuasion. For in the sense that "the kingdom of God is not meat and drink," (Rom. xiv. 16-18) neither is it water; "but righteousness, and peace, and joy in the Holy Ghost." It were well if all Baptists were of Spurgeon's mind. There would then be MUCH less temptation to special pleadings, misrepresentation of persons and things, unchristian arts of proselytism, and (to use Bunyan's description) less "breach of love and taking off Christians from the more weighty things of God, and to make them quarrel and have heart-burnings one against another," etc. And consequently so much less sin and more blessing from God. But as matters appear, it seems unlikely for long yet that such a Christian spirit will prevail among and rule over the Close Communionist section. From before and since Bunyan's time it has continued the same, and seems in no degree abating. The more also it is borne with, the bolder and more zealous in proselytizing improprieties it becomes.

I have taken occasion from our recent short and decisive controversy to reproduce my lecture on that subject. The publication is specially intended for the benefit of my own congregations and others of the neighbourhood interested, and is a contribution to the cause of truth, considered desirable, and it is hoped may be, by the divine blessing, of some real service in exhibiting the wrong things said and done in connection with the ordinance of baptism. There having been no regular ministry settled here until recently, many of my own people, with others, from lack of opportunities, etc., will doubtless not have that particular knowledge on this and other things that is desirable. And there are some here whose great ambition is to unsettle minds from what we do most assuredly believe to be the faith once delivered to the saints. Besides in these days of movement to and fro our young people and others are liable to be exposed elsewhere to the same influences, which it is the duty and wisdom of ministers and parents to anticipate and properly provide against.

Although I have dealt throughout with all plainness, and with censure when that appeared needful, (in which, brethren, as you have seen, I have always furnished the materials for your own independent judgment) I harbour no unkindly feelings towards our Baptist brethren. That they generally believe themselves in the right in their views and zeal there can be no doubt. Though I need hardly say that sincerely and strongly believing ourselves in the right is no proof at all of rightness. Romanists and many others enthusiastically believe as much in regard to great errors. Mr. Bunyan's and Mr. Spurgeon's views, which I have quoted you on the practical bearings of the subject, I cordially subscribe to as mine also, as they are of our church and others. If I have said anything unpleasant to those we differ from, I have only done it because the truth unfolded in the interests of truth has been of that nature to their feelings. We wish them well. Grace, mercy and peace be upon all—Baptists, Episcopalians, Methodists, Congregationalists, and all others of any name under heaven who love the Lord Jesus Christ in sincerity. And may he have saving mercy upon the multitudes that love him not.

> Pray that Jerusalem may have
>   Peace and felicity:
> Let them that love thee and thy peace
>   Have still prosperity.
>
> Therefore I wish that peace may still
>   Within thy walls remain,
> And ever may thy palaces
>   Prosperity retain.
>
> Now, for my friends' and brethren's sakes,
>   Peace be in thee, I'll say,
> And for the house of God our Lord,
>   I'll seek thy good alway.
>
> And blessed be his glorious name
>   To all eternity:
> The whole earth let his glory fill,
>   Amen, so let it be.

APPENDIX

I.

I HAVE shown my readers specimens of the policy of misrepresentation pursued in books issued by the Baptist Publication Societies. I will add here some further exhibitions of the same in reference to ourselves, as many of you having been eye-witnesses of the facts will be able to judge correctly from your own knowledge. The best of men, from frailty or misled by others, do make mistakes; hence it would lack not only Christian charity and forbearance, but common justice to make much of isolated cases of that nature, which might be most unintentional. But the following will be seen to be of a different type of spirit altogether. With reference to our meetings here in December, etc., several communications thereafter appeared in local newspapers at a distance highly charged with gross misrepresentations in the Baptist interest. But not till the 9th March, did anything appear in the *Canadian Baptist*—the leading Baptist paper of the Province. Again a second appeared there on the 23rd, and another a month after. I sent two replies, the first of which was published in it, but preceded by a private course (which I will yet explain) tending to its exclusion; and the second was refused a place on a transparently unworthy pretext. This letter I sent in consequence to our own denominational paper, which appeared in its issue of 5th May. From all which it will appear that the *management* of the Close Communionist church paper, in its sectarian policy, affords all facility for Baptist correspondence, however loaded with odious personal misrepresentations of other denominations, and then protects them from exposure by refusing a place to replies in correction; which protection seems to be expected (as it may) by its correspondents, from experience, judging from the fearless length to which they have ventured in our own case. As the Latin proverb has it, *ex uno disce multibus*—" From one example learn many." The following was my communication to our paper, containing my reply, refused publication in the *Canadian Baptist*.

Editor BRITISH AMERICAN PRESBYTERIAN:

DEAR SIR,—I will thank you if you can spare the space for the following communication of mine to the *Canadian Baptist*, *refused* a place in its columns. After waiting till after three issues, without its appearance there, I wrote a friend in Toronto to call on and ask the editor if he intended to publish it, who has informed me that he considered it "useless" to do so, "as there was now *no question* of *fact*, but merely of opinion." Now, any one who reads it will see the very opposite to be the case, and that the editor of the leading paper of the Baptist denomination does not think it beneath him to use a very unworthy pretext to avoid doing an act of common (not to say Christian) justice ; and that to a minister of another denomination against whom *himself* has issued to his readers all over the Province as gross a misrepresentation of facts as ever pen inscribed. For *certain*, as he, of course, could see, my reply *is* on questions of *fact*, and *not opinions at all*, and I, the accused, have not yet been, and will not be permitted, so far as his power extends, a word on them in my own defence in his readers' hearing. The other communication of mine referred to at the beginning of this refused one, did not refer to the same matters. Nor was its admission unattended with difficulties. On the 9th of March a long communication from an anonymous Baptist correspondent appeared in that paper, literally packed with gross misrepresentations of facts (no less than fifteen), to which a reply of mine was sent at once, and tardily inserted, and was preceded by a remarkable private procedure towards myself on the part of the *Canadian Baptist* management, the direct and immediate result of which, had it it been successful, (which it might have been, *unknown* to me), would have also thoroughly prevented *that* reply from appearing. The disclosure of that procedure I will request the favour of your insertion in a subsequent issue, your space being too largely drawn upon at this time already. The *genuine reason* of the policy (of Romish hue) in refusing publication to the following, will be apparent, on reading it, to any acquainted with the spirit and ways of Close Communionism. And I am, dear sir, yours respectfully,

JOHN BETHUNE.

Chesley, 29th April, 1876.

To the Editor of the CANADIAN BAPTIST:

DEAR SIR,—My reply in your issue of the 30th ultimo, to the communication under the fictitious signature, " M.," in yours of the 9th preceding, exhibits some of his *many* gross misrepresentations of fact, sufficient to show that whoever your correspondent may be, he sadly lacks the spirit of truth; who instinctively felt it desirable to screen himself from the view of those who know the facts, by withholding his own name, while he has no such delicacy in abundantly repeating mine—like the disreputable many who do under cover of the night what they shrink from in the day time when seen and known. I observe also in yours of the 23rd ultimo, another communication, "Explanatory," of which I am the subject by name, the writer of which signs himself " P.M.," who appears from it to be, without doubt, the Rev. Peter McDonald, St. Mary's. Like the former, it is also a gross misrepresentation of facts. If these communications are specimens of other accounts that appear in your columns, your readers must be often grievously misled.

Mr. McDonald confines his observations to a lecture I delivered in my own church here, on the evening of the 16th December last, on Confessions of Faith, and to a meeting in the Baptist church the following evening, in which himself took a prominent part. To these observations and the *facts* as they *actually* occurred, permit me, Sir, to direct the attention of your readers. My lecture on Confessions of Faith was delivered to a large audience, who were most attentive and orderly to the close. At the beginning for fifteen or twenty minutes I read and remarked upon the very unjust strictures in a communication by " Ottawa " in your issue of 28th Oct. last, on our Presbyterian Church and its Confession of Faith, which was placed by you, as worthy of the position, in your first page, under the section permanently headed, " THE BAPTIST PULPIT." I then entered upon my lecture. (1) In regard to it Mr. McDonald says, it " was mainly based on two positions. 1st. The Confession is not ' a fetter,'—an obvious hit at Mr. Macdonnell. 2nd. The Confession of Faith settles doctrinal questions and prevents various opinions on the same theological points." This account is quite incorrect. When I spoke of a " fetter " was when reading " Ottawa's " article in the *Canadian Baptist*, where that expression occurs, and before entering on my lecture. The " obvious hit " is drawn from his own imagination. And what he calls my second position of lecture is drawn entirely from the same source. I neither said nor believe that Confessions prevent various theological opinions, etc. The expressions are *his own* and not mine. What he means by " settling doctrinal questions " I don't quite understand. (2) Mr. McD. says, " He (Mr. Bethune) succeeded at the close to get Mr. Carnes up beside him,"—evidently something very bad on Mr. B.'s part. The fact is as follows: When I closed my lecture, I invited Mr. Carnes, who was present, to make any reply he might desire. He then came forward to the platform, replied, and sat down of his own choice on a chair there. Such was my "succeeding," and the way of it. (8) Mr. McDonald adds, "and as the latter (Mr. Carnes) had said, and repeated it there, that the Baptists have no Confession of Faith, Mr. B. raised a pamphlet to the face of the former, saying, 'There is a Baptist Confession of Faith, and patronized by your own Spurgeon.'" These, in regard to me, are flagrant falsehoods. When Mr. Carnes had replied, I lifted a small book from the table, rose, and said to *the meeting:* "You have heard Mr. Carnes say, 'the Baptists have *always* and *all along* contended *against* Confessions of Faith.' I have a small book in my hand I got by last mail from the Baptist Book Room, Toronto. I will read its title. It is called 'The Baptist Confession of Faith,'" Immediately on this Mr. Carnes reached out his hand quickly, saying, "Let me see it please." I handed it to him without a word, and waited its return. Then HE SAID (not I), "O that's Spurgeon's Confession he made for his own congregation." I replied, "Well, I will read a little more," which, opening it, I did as follows: "We, the ministers and messengers of, and concerned for upwards of one hundred of Baptized Churches . . . being met together in London, from the 3rd of the 7th month to the 11th of the same, 1689, to consider," etc. I also read from Mr. Spurgeon's short preface to it in which he speaks of it as "this excellent list of doctrines which was subscribed unto by the Baptist ministers in 1689." And I explained that it was throughout nearly word for word a repetition of our Westminster Confession, excepting on Baptism and the section on the civil magistrate, and one or two other modifications in the way of omission. I also produced two other present day Baptist Confessions, and next evening presented another. These, Sir, are the real facts. I did not lift a pamphlet to Mr. C.'s face, nor speak at all, as Mr. McD. alleges. (4) Near the end of his "Explanatory" to you, he says of that Baptist Confession of 1689, that next evening he himself "explained the circumstances under which it originated, viz.: that it was framed in the reign of Charles the II. as a vindication of a Pædo-baptist maligned people." Just so. He did say so, and other things equally contrary to fact. You are aware, Mr. Editor, that Charles II. died in A.D. 1685, or four years *before* that Confession was framed in 1689; also that it was framed the year after King William III. had taken the place of James II. Had Mr. McDonald told your readers (which he omitted) *the date* of that Confession, a number of them could see his misstatements for themselves. I supply it now.

At the close of my lecture and meeting, Mr. Carnes said that I had dishonestly suppressed parts of "Ottawa's" article in the *Canadian Baptist*, and invited the people to a meeting next evening in the Baptist church, when he said that that article would be read over from beginning to end (one and a quarter columns), and my dishonesty would be seen, and my lecture on Confessions would be reviewed. Next evening in the Baptist church, Mr. Carnes was in the chair. After opening the meeting, the first thing he said was that the article by "Ottawa" in the *Canadian Baptist* would be *dispensed with*, and Rev. Peter McDonald would address the meeting. Mr. McD. began by a criticism of certain Greek words of the baptism controversy—*louo, nipto, kataduno, bapto, baptizo, buthizo*, etc. (5) In his "Explanatory" to you he says, "Having understood during a former visit that Mr. Bethune had declared publicly, when *baptizo* signifies to submerge, that it is in the sense of to sink to the bottom, I named various Greek words," etc. On this I beg to say, first, he did not make any such statement at all at that meeting; and next, I NEVER declared publicly or privately any such thing, and don't believe, nor ever did, any such nonsense about *baptizo*.

(6) He further says, "The gentleman (that is, Mr. Bethune) favoured the writer (Rev. P. McDonald) with *early* and *continued* interruptions." I answer that the man who could pen that statement in the face of the facts, which he knew, is capable of anything in the shape of slander. He began his observations before seven o'clock and closed after nine. For about twenty minutes at the beginning he went on discussing the Greek words before mentioned of Baptistic controversy. I rose (being on the platform), stated that we had been invited to hear that article of "Ottawa" in the *Canadian Baptist* read all through, and my dishonest suppression of parts of it exposed, and a review of my lecture on Confessions of Faith, but the *Canadian Baptist's* article was dismissed, and instead of a review of my lecture we were getting one on Baptism, a quite different subject. I called on the lecturer to come to the subjects promised us, and sat down. Mr. Carnes, chairman, said I was interrupting Mr. McDonald, who proceeded; but now dwelt (not more than fifteen or twenty minutes) on our Westminster Confession, and then came again to the subject of immersion *versus* sprinkling, on which thereafter he occupied the remaining hour and a-half, and even then had no sign of ceasing, till I rose and asked if it was intended that I should get an opportunity of reply. Once again during his discussion of the latter subject I rose and spoke as before, respectfully calling on him to come to the promised subjects of the evening. This Mr. Carnes said was interrupting him, and he went on on Baptism to the end. Once on my seat beside him, when he gave "is" as the mean-

ing of the Hebrew word " Haya," on which he placed weight, I answered, " It literally signifies 'has been.'" Another time, on the Greek word *louo* which he dwelt on, I mentioned on my seat that the Baptist New Testament translation renders it " to wash." At two different times I respectfully requested the name of the small book he read a large number of professed quotations from Paedo-baptist writers from, and each time he said *fiercely*, "O I can do that!" but did not give it. *Such* were *literally* all my *interruptions*, which no honourable man would characterize as he has chosen to do, especially also considering what I have not yet related. (7) The points he dwelt on on our Confession as a "fetter" in his view, he states were its doctrines on "foreordination and baptism." (My lecture was not at all one proving our doctrines Scriptural, which would take many lectures from their number; but the nature, uses, and necessity of Confessions, considered as containing what are believed and acknowledged by those whose they are to be Scriptural). He sagaciously, however, omits to inform your readers of his other " fetters," which were, that our doctrines that "faith is a saving grace " and that "the first day of the week is the Sabbath," are contrary to Scripture and can not be proven therefrom. Mr. Carnes took the same position on the latter, publicly in his church some weeks before. These points Mr. McD. referred to, I showed, when my reply came, to be taught in Mr. Spurgeon's Catechism and the Baptist Confession of 1689, etc. (8) But now as to his and Mr. Carnes's conduct. The evening before, in my own church, when I was replying to Mr. Carnes' reply—showing and reading the Baptist Confessions mentioned -he constantly called to me from his seat, and often rose up to say something, till the meeting could not stand it, and from all parts called him to order. Next evening Mr. McD. *all through* his observations directed his remarks to myself in brow-beating style, calling on me then and there to answer him to each thing, yes or no, giving out challenges, and saying "he did not care for one of my coat," etc., etc. When I was replying at the end, he kept *constantly leaping up on his feet* beside me interposing objections, or calling out to me from his seat *every sentence I uttered;* Mr. Carnes helping him in this. I never witnessed such conduct in my life. (9) In his ". Explanatory," *without stating that I spoke in reply at the end*, he intersperses distorted statements of mine *as made throughout* his own lecture, no doubt to make them appear as interruptions. One of these is that when he challenged me I declined, saying, " I have enough of it." When such words were used by me was *after* I had finished my reply, and been challenged again, Mr. McD. saying he would be ready to meet me or any in Canada next morning at six `o'clock. I replied that my subject was Confessions of Faith, that I had lectured on it, and they had a night also in reply, such as their reply was. Still they challenged. I then said, "Since you force me to speak my feelings, I may tell you I would feel myself degraded. in entering on a controversy with men who have conducted themselves so disgracefully as you have done. If I wanted to crush the feelings of the Baptists here, I could not do better than accept your challenge, but I have no pleasure in that. Your gross rudeness and unfairness itself would ruin your cause in your hands. And to do the Baptists justice, I may say, I don't regard you as fair representatives of their ministers, though I consider their position on baptism wrong. That is my answer to you. I have had enough of it to-night for a while."

Want of space prevents me from adding further particulars.

Please to insert this, my reply to Mr. Macdonald's, and excuse its length (which I have condensed as much as possible), as you know it necessarily takes more space to correct misstatements than to make them. Allow me also in a sentence, to add that I consider it a very unjust and demoralizing practice to send or to publish personal accusations of others, especially of another denomination, without the personal signature of the accuser. I am, dear sir, yours respectfully, JOHN BETHUNE.

Chesley, 3rd April, 1876.

The following from me appeared in the same paper on the 19th May :—

Editor BRITISH AMERICAN PRESBYTERIAN :

SIR,—The brethren who read my communication in your issue of the 5th inst. would see the very gross misrepresentations of myself, etc., by the Rev. P. McDonald, Baptist minister, published to his readers all over the province by the editor of the *Canadian Baptist*, in his issue of the 23rd March ; and how groundless his reason for refusing that reply of mine a place in his columns, viz.: that it did not refer to questions of *fact*,— a reason which any reader who knows what an account of facts is, would at once perceive to be as untrue as his refusal to publish my statement, in my own defence from odious vilification of what actually occurred in the meetings in question, was unjust and a gross violation on his as well as his correspondent's part of the ninth commandment—"Thou shalt not bear false witness against thy neighbour." Meanwhile, his readers having seen no correction of Mr. McDonald's representations will, of course, regard them as *unquestioned* facts, his being a minister of their own and I of another denomination, and the matters being of Baptist interest, will, from their natural and strong bias, strengthen that conviction.

I stated in my last communication that a former reply of mine to a previous anonymous communication in the *Canadian*

Baptist was admitted, but under peculiar difficulties, which I will thank you to allow me now to explain. I get several papers of different names weekly, and for years, without an issue not coming duly to hand. Since last fall I happen to be a subscriber to the *Canadian Baptist*, and always received my copy weekly at the usual time till that of March 2nd, which was not forwarded to me from the *Canadian Baptist* office. I was not aware then that the editor had received immediately before this a communication from a Baptist correspondent here, in which myself by name, figured prominently, and so looked on the non-arrival of copy, though unusual, as accidental. The next issue, however, (of March 9) did not come to hand either, although on both occasions I learned the copies for the Baptist subscribers had come as usual. Considering that several communications from the Baptist side had recently been appearing in local papers at some distance from here, highly charged with gross misrepresentations to those who did not know the matters, to relieve the unhappiness felt by that side at their ill-success in meetings here in January and December, I suspected there might be something of this nature at the bottom of the non-forwarding of my copies. I consequently sent a card to the editor, requesting him to rectify for the future, and to send me the two back numbers that had not come. A week afterwards I received these, when, lo, in the last one was an article of one and a half columns, full from beginning to end of the most unscrupulous misrepresentations of facts, in which by name perpetually I was presented in a very odious light. Of these, *nine* were direct, the things alleged having been neither said nor done by me, literally or virtually. *Other six* were gross misrepresentations, by concealment of facts well known to every one here, and by distortions in what is stated. The w. ole was prepared by no novice in the art, with much care to get in as much into the space as possible. The reception and publication of this, *seemed* now to have been *the reason*, in the circumstances, *why* the issue containing it was not sent to me. If I did not see that issue, I would not see and so would not reply to that communication, and the Baptist readers would get the benefit of it, in that case, as an account not called in question. Even when one of another denomination should reply to a Baptist's misstatements, they will be inclined to trust to the veracity of their own representative and his more agreeable affirmations. How much more when then there is no contrary account? In rural districts in particular it is very rare if ever that any is a subscriber to that paper except Baptists. Of course this is nowhere better known than in the C. B. office. Such is the case here. Baptists would not inform me of it, and if I had not had my attention drawn to other local communications before (of which the Canadian Baptist office away in Toronto would know nothing), I would easily not have thought of caring so much for the copies that did not come as to send for the back numbers. In any case a *delay of reply* was certain, and might be considerable, and in these matters, likely to render it useless, as past date, though the misrepresentations would leave *their* impression.

Having first seen the article on the 16th, I mailed a reply on the 18th ; I also wrote a friend in Toronto the circumstances mentioned, expressing my apprehension of the Editor's adopting a policy of now *delaying its publication* as long as possible, and requesting him should it not appear in the first issue (on the 23rd), to call on and ask the Editor when he intended to insert it. This he did and informed me that he said it was not received in time for that week's issue, and was afraid it would be *crowded out of the next* by matter in type, (so much in type *ten* days before for a weekly paper !) but in the issue after that I was to expect it. He mentioned further that the Editor explained as the reason of my copies not being sent, that my name had *accidentally* fallen out of the *printed* mailing list of subscribers, but was reinserted when I wrote him. Just fancy a subscriber's name *falling* out of a printed list, long before his subscription time terminated, accidentally too, and just at the time, and no other, when a vilifying communication in Baptist interests had appeared against him.

Meanwhile on that same 23rd, the fourth day after my reply had come to his hand, he published a second series of vilifications of myself, etc., this time from the Rev. Mr. McDonald, which as it alluded to the communication of the 9th, could only have been a short time in his hands ; while my reply to the first was apparently not to see the light before the 6th April, a month after the first one appeared. At the same tardy rate (different from the measure to the Baptist assailants, who as yet had it all their own way) should I next reply to Mr. McD's, it would not be seen till about May, *if at all.* Honourable editors *make* room at once for defences from personal accusations made in their columns ; but here the C. B. office first directly causes *by its own action* delay of my reply (no thanks to it if it was not greater), and now that it is forwarded, means to take its time though the accusations were particularly flagrant in number and nature. In these circumstances I at once wrote a brief communication to the Editor, expressing my disappointment at the so long proposed postponement, referred to the copies not coming to me as singular, and requested him if he could not publish mine in next issue to publish this short one meanwhile. In the next issue, however, (the 30th) my first now appeared, not the short one. Three days after that I mailed my reply to the Rev. P. McDonald's, with what result your readers have been already informed ; also the same day (about three weeks later) that my friend called to ask if he meant to publish it and was told, No ; he published a third reflecting on me from another Baptist correspondent ; to which of course it was useless to reply after the refusal of my last. My friend's words in note to me on that refusal are in full as follows—(The Editor of the C. B.,) " Mr. Muir says that as there is now no question of *fact*, but merely of *opinion*, it is useless to continue the controversy. He inserted an acknowledgment of having *received* it, he says, in last issue, and thinks that is enough." Here, besides stating it does not deal with *facts*, he refers to the length of time "the controversy" had been in his paper, and makes *that* an *excuse* for the *suppression*. So the policy of delaying my preparation of my first reply (if not preventing it altogether), and then of its publication, is made serviceable in not allowing me to defend myself from new misrepresentations. Only *two days* after I saw the first of 9th March, my reply to it was mailed, and the 3rd day after that was published I sent him my second. So the delaying has been all his, and I have got but one reply to one communication, and none to the others that followed.

Such are the Editor and Baptist correspondence of the *Canadian Baptist;* such the matter and manner in which their unsuspecting readers are confirmed in their distinctive Baptist ideas, and prejudiced to dislike and despise infant-baptists and "baby sprinkling ;" and such are examples of the way other denominations are vilified and gagged as far as may be. *Sed magna est veritas et prevalebit.* " Every plant which my heavenly Father hath not planted shall be rooted up."

Hoping the nature of the matters disclosed will excuse the lengthened occupation of your space, I am, dear sir, yours respectfully, JOHN BETHUNE.

Chesley, 8th *May,* 1876.

The writer of the communication signed "M." in the *Canadian Baptist* of 9th March, referred to just now in mine to the *British American Presbyterian,* I privately learned to have been Duncan McGillivray, a zealous Baptist here of middle age, and of great religious profession. Meeting him afterwards he acknowledged to my inquiry that he was its author. I will give you some specimens from it of his method of advancing his cause.—1. Referring to my criticism of the article in the *Canadian Baptist* of 28th Oct. last, at the meeting of my lecture on Confessions of Faith, he states that I " *strung* some quotations from the article together, *in such* a way, as to make the writer say that the Presbyterian church was a huge mass of hollow rottenness."

That is to say, I greatly misrepresented that writer, who, it is implied by this, said nothing of the kind. Now let my reader turn again to the PREFACE of this treatise (page ix.), where he will see the quotation containing those words "a huge mass of hollow rottenness" and *others* no better, with their connections, and judge whether I misrepresented. —2. At that meeting of mine I refrained throughout from any reference whatever to *the subject of Baptism*, as all the large audience well know, but confined myself solely to 'Confessions of Faith.' (And Rev. Mr. Carnes while "fearlessly" and zealously pressing his views of Baptism and our degeneracy for the past three months, had as yet received on it no word of opposition.) Yet D. McG., in his account of my lecture, after one sentence, to represent what I said on the Westminster Confession, adds, that I "also maintained that the Baptists have not a claim to the name (Baptists) exclusively, as he (Mr. Bethune) claimed that the Presbyterians were Baptists." He then continues, "On the following evening in the Baptist church, the Rev. P. McDonald, who was present on the occasion of the lecture, reviewed the Confession," and "dwelt at some length on Baptism." Now besides that he was aware I had not touched on Baptism, as he was present, he also heard me that next evening complain that while we had all been invited to hear only a review of my lecture on Confessions of Faith and the C. B. article, we were getting instead a controversial lecture on Baptism, on which I had not spoken at all. The people also he knew, were dissatisfied, among the several other scandals of that evening, with this unbecoming breach of faith. He, however, by this invention about my having discussed that question makes Rev. P. McDonald appear justified by my example. Six weeks after that, viz. 27th Jan., at the very beginning of my *Lecture on Infant Baptism* (see p. 1), I made that claim about the name of Baptist (he being present), and this he coolly transfers away back to the meeting of 16th December.—3. Of a discourse on Sabbath, 23rd January, in his own church, he relates, "This sermon touched Mr. Bethune in a very tender place, as he could not refrain from *calling aloud* for the name of the book from which the quotations (from Paedobaptist writers) were read." By this he obviously intended the readers of the *Canadian*

Baptist to understand that I had so "called aloud" *during the delivery* of the "sermon," when those quotations were read, and was very irreverent and boisterous. I will give now the matter *exactly as* it occurred. *After* Mr. C. had *closed his meeting* by pronouncing the benediction, and *when* the people were all on their feet and going out at the door, I went forward to him and respectfully said that I would thank him for the name of that book. Compare now the facts with his account!—4. Having been refused the name of the book in question, (and Rev. P. McDonald having refused me on the 17th December that of the one he used similarly,) I resolved now to give an exposure of their misquotations, in connection with my already intimated lecture on the early history of infant baptism on the following Thursday evening; and put up a bill to that effect in the village. After quoting that bill Duncan McG. goes on to relate of my lecture, "The ONLY part *of the above 'bill of fare'* that the reverend gentleman fulfilled, after exhausting about forty-five minutes in personal abuse of Mr. Carnes, was the FIRST item, viz.;—the early history of infant baptism." That is to say, I neither showed nor attempted to show any misquotations of Paedobaptist writers, but entirely occupied the time instead before beginning the "history of infant baptism" with abuse of Mr. C.; and this of course (as the Baptist readers were to infer) because no misquotations *could* be shown. Now that lecture my readers have in the first part of this book. If you will please turn back to it, (p. 12 to 86,) you will see again the large number I brought out in regard to Baxter, Wesley, Clarke, Matthew Henry, Dwight, Doddridge, the Greek Church, etc. All these were shown *before* entering on the "history;" so that the forty-five minutes were occupied largely with somethings more than Mr. C. 5-7. Immediately after that statement, about my lecture, he next describes Mr. Carnes' reply to it on the following Wednesday evening in the Baptist Church, of which he relates: "Mr. Carnes had shown where all this animus came from, by reading from Dr. Cramp's History the following." Here he gives a long quotation from Dr. C. about the intolerance, 200 years ago, of the Presbyterian Clergy, Scottish Parliament, and the 'Solemn League and Covenant.' After which he added, (note this!) "He, Mr. Carnes, read from the *Confession of Faith* on the same subject (which, by the way, Mr. Bethune denied to be the *Westminster* Confession, to which he subscribed, but when shown to him in private afterwards he acknowledged his error)." The cool audacity of the gross falsehood after falsehood in the above is astonishing! The facts were these: Mr. Carnes, in his difficulties, devoted that evening chiefly to raking up material from Cramp, etc., to shew the persecuting spirit of Presbyterians past and present. After reading that portion referred to from Cramp, he next told the audience he would now read them a part of the WESTMINSTER CONFESSION, that I had subscribed to, vowed to teach, etc., in which they would see taught there the intolerance Cramp referred to. After he had read a few lines, I (being present) rose and said: "That is not the Westminster Confession you are reading, but 'The Solemn League and Covenant,' which is a quite different document, and was not subscribed to by me, nor is a document of our church at all." He affirmed in reply that it was the Westminster Confession. I requested him to hand it to me and I would show it was not. He at first would not give it to me, but after some manœuvring on his part I went up beside him, got it, and showed it to the audience to be as I had said. He then maintained that the 'Solemn League and Covenant' was a part of the *Westminster Confession!* While all who know anything of these matters know that it is not; and that the Reformed Presbyterians are the only denomination of all Presbyterians who subscribe that document, and hence are called "Covenanters" to distinguish them from us and others. Besides, that same evening I showed him, and the audience, the Westminster Confession itself,—another document. Yet, though all this was witnessed by hundreds, and it has never yet been denied that what he read was the 'Solemn League and Covenant,' D. McG., a month afterwards relates: That I denied *The Westminster Confession* to be the Westminster Confession. And to make this beyond all controversy adds that I "in private afterwards acknowledged I was in error in denying that what he read from was that Confession!" In "private" or public I never thought of, or acknowledged any such thing. But D. McG. does not mention at all that it was the Solemn League and Covenant, Mr. C.

read. To specify that document and tell *the truth* would have spoiled his object. Besides these various misrepresentations of his I have referred to, there are several others in that communication of like nature. For instance, one remarkable feature of the meeting just mentioned was the fact that, and the remarkable manner in which Mr. C. intimated at the beginning that I would be allowed *no reply*, and that when he did so again, towards the close, the whole meeting, excepting a very small proportion, rose up and retired from the church in a body, while he was speaking. Yet D. McG. represents me as making a lengthened reply, and specifies the topics also, which he transfers from my own meeting of the previous Thursday, (and not without gross misrepresentations of them also,) then returning, further on, to this subject he repeats of this meeting of Mr. Carnes', " On the Wednesday evening he (Mr. Bethune) *concludes* a *long address* with the following appeal." He then ascribes to me words I neither expressed on that, nor on any Wednesday evening, nor at that or any other meeting! He concludes his account by expressing the hope that some here " may ultimately realize that they are saved by faith and not ' by praying.' " The last two words he puts between quotation commas, and are an allusion to Mr. Carnes's doctrine that salvation is not to be prayed for ; and, considering the connection, insinuate the untruth that I teach that ' they are saved by prayer without faith.' Now, let my readers recollect that hundreds here—of my own congregation, and others—will read these statements of mine, who were eyewitnesses of all the facts referred to, and know what is true of them, and would cease to respect me were I to state falsehood. I don't write with a fictitious signature like " M." under which D. McG. concealed himself.

II.

In the *Bruce Reporter* of Kincardine (a local paper forty miles distant) there appeared two lengthy communications from here, on the 3rd and 17th of February, respectively, full of misrepresentations of the same nature as those just explained. A reply from me appeared in its issue of the

9th of March, pointing out some of the more flagrant. In the end of the same month a short one appeared from Duncan McGillivray (but not with his personal signature), in which, after a sophistical reference to a statement in mine, he concluded by asking his readers to consider the arrogance of the man (myself) "who signs himself 'THE Presbyterian Minister of Chesley,' while there is another Presbyterian minister here, who attends to his own business, and preaches his own sermons." The other minister referred to, I may say, belongs to the United Presbyterian denomination of the United States, and was not here till some time after this correspondence in that paper began. On the occasion already mentioned, when I met D. McG., and heard from himself, in answer to my inquiry, that he was also the author of the communication in the *Canadian Baptist*, I repeated the above quotation, and said to him, "When you sent that to the *Bruce Reporter* you knew well that the other Presbyterian minister came here only two or three weeks before you wrote, and that when I wrote my communication to it previously, there was no Presbyterian minister here but myself, then or before; also that, in those letters to which mine was a reply, I was spoken of under that title, as *the* Presbyterian minister here. Of this you mentioned nothing, but wrote to produce the impression that another Presbyterian minister was here all along, and that I in arrogance, ignored his presence. Yet you knew perfectly this was not the case. How could you make such a statement I wish to know?' To this he replied with a smile and silence. I pressed him on the meanness and sin of such conduct and his religious profession. Still he said not a word. (Observe also what *himself* had written a few weeks earlier in the beginning of his communication in the *Canadian Baptist*. Referring to the "discussion" he was about to relate, he said as follows,— "It arose between THE Presbyterian minister of this place, on the one hand, and the Baptist minister on the other." It happened also that this appeared in the C. B., and mine in the *Bruce Reporter* each on the *same* date, 9th March.) I said to him further, 'You also added that that other minister "attends to his own business and preaches his own sermons," by which you plainly meant your readers to understand that I don't do these things. Now I want to know what grounds you have for saying that I don't preach my own sermons?' He gave no answer. I pressed him for one, referring to the baseness of his spirit that could deliberately fabricate and give out to the many readers of a newspaper such a slander in hope by such means to aid his Baptist cause! He then answered: "I did not say *you* did not preach your own sermons." This answer I pointed out was a mere evasion of the words he used, which he evidently intended to convey that meaning, and would certainly be so understood. A word more, however, on the subject he would not say; and that simply because he had no grounds for the statement, which was as entire a fabrication as the other about my signature, and his many others a few weeks earlier in the *Canadian Baptist*.

I have now exhibited specimens of Rev. Mr. McDonald's and Mr. McGillivray's methods of aiding their cause when in difficulties, of covering up the deficiencies of their own side of things, misrepresenting those they oppose, and trying to make the worse appear the better by the unchristian genius of bearing unwearied false-witness; also their *Church* paper's methods of assisting the same unhallowed policy by freely circulating such misrepresentations to its readers, at the same time quietly, at the right time for concealment, keeping back our subscription copy containing these, and afterwards refusing to publish our self-defence and true account, on the pretext that *our* account of the *facts* was merely our "opinion" of what we and the others did or did not *say* and *do*!

In the interest of true religion and public morality I have also brought out the real names of those who have so acted, as many have so little of the fear of God and regard for truth (with profession of much zeal for it) as willingly to go any length in false-witness under cover of concealment, as fictitious signatures, who would be more careful if their names were given as publicly as the names *they* give without stint or delicacy of those against whom they say all manner of evil falsely. Many of my readers know the facts in question and can judge the merits for themselves. Nor have I given of those communications more than one half of their misrepresentations, as all would take up too much space.

But besides these there were several other letters of like

kind, all of which with one exception (of a mingled nature) were of similar character, and all but one in papers which have few or no readers here. Five appeared in the *Bruce Reporter*, Kincardine, all the way, in the neighbourhood of which are many Baptists. To the readers of that paper the people here, not Baptists, were described (without personal signature as usual) as "the great unwashed,"—an expression applied to the scum of cities; though it is but true to say they will compare favorably for respectability of character and behaviour with any township in the Province. Of our meetings in December they were told that the Baptist ministers "overthrew the Presbyterian minister's Confessions of Faith, *the paternity of which he was anxious to ascribe to the Baptist Church!*" And that in the meeting on the 2nd February the Baptist minister "read out *a part of the Westminster Confession of Faith;*" that I then "got up and denied that as the Confession of Faith, and explained that it *was the* Shorter and Longer Catechism," etc.! This is the incident about the "Solemn League and Covenant," about which the writer (like D. McGillivray, three weeks later in the *Canadian Baptist*) did not give a whisper. Such is the style throughout. Among the rest they were informed of my character that where I was stationed before, the people there "were excited against me on account of an idiosyncrasy with a female Sunday school class of mine." Satan could not devise a more complete falsehood than this. In the first place, I had no female or other "Sunday" or week day class; and next, *there never has been*, in my lifetime, anywhere, any excitement or complaint against me, in private or public, for any impropriety with or towards females, less or more.

III.

In the beginning of February an incident occurred I will now notice. On the 4th of that month there appeared in the *Telescope* of Walkerton, a reply from me to a communication there the week before from its local correspondent here—a Baptist—who referring to our meetings in December, while admitting that the Baptist ministers acted "disgracefully," felt disposed to ascribe to me, without reason, a share in that blame. I explained the facts, and among other details remarked as follows:— "Different leading Baptists have distinctly told me that they could find no fault with my spirit or conduct at either meeting, but were ashamed of their own ministers." The end of the week following, a short letter, signed by "Donald McGregor, clerk of Baptist church," and "R. F. Atkinson, chairman of meeting," appeared in three local papers, and afterwards in a fourth, stating that at a meeting of their church that statement of mine, quoted above, was brought forward, and it continued: "A committee was appointed to investigate the matter, but the minister of the Presbyterian church would not give the names of any of the parties he says told him so. Now we as a church emphatically deny and repudiate the same entirely."

Well, be it so, but that did not alter the fact. However I will now explain a little on this of details. In the beginning of that week two men called on me at my house whom I did not know, but on inquiry learned their names, one of which was Mr. Atkinson, the same, I suppose, whose signature appeared to that letter. And note this. Neither of them stated or hinted in any way that they were a committee or sent by any to me; which surely in their duty as a deputation, and if they wished to succeed, they should have done; but they appeared only to have come of their own individual option. Also Mr. Atkinson, who was *the* speaker, was so very rude that twice I informed him that unless he were more civil in his behaviour our interview would close. Had the desire been that I would refuse the names that they might publish that, they could not have, in the nature of the case, adopted a course more likely to succeed in this. I told them that what I had stated in the *Telescope* was absolutely true, but that I did not consider I ought to give those parties' names to any who chose to ask me; that their motive in asking them, I believed, could only be to show them hostility, not for saying what was untrue; for their ministers' conduct on the occasion was in everybody's mouth; but for disclosing their feelings on the subject to me. And I added that it must be very difficult to make them (my visitors) ashamed, if they were not themselves ashamed of their ministers' behaviour. This last sentence I again repeated, and then they each said they were not present at the meeting (17th Dec.). So those deputed to call on me were two who did not personally know the facts in question. One of my elders, Mr. J. McL., happening to be with me on a casual visit, was present at this interview, and knows the accuracy of this account. I must add another feature, for which I am sorry, as from my little personal acquaintance and what I had heard of the Baptist brother concerned in it, I had a heart regard for him, and still have, as I believe he acted through fear (yet sinfully), and would not have done it had he been free from that temptation. Of his name I will therefore meanwhile just mention the first part.

Not long after the December meetings, A. — — being in the village, I happened to see him and we conversed about them. He then voluntarily expressed to me those words referred to. The week after that letter appeared on this subject, I met him again in the village, and the following conversation occurred between us. I inquired if he was present at the meeting in the Baptist Church last week, that sent that letter to the papers. He answered, yes. I asked him if *he* voted for that letter. He said, he did. I then said, " And how could you do so, Archibald, when you knew that yourself for one had made that statement to me, which it denied ? " He inquired when he said so ; and I reminded him of the time and place. He replied, " Mr. Bethune, I told you at the time I was dull of hearing. I did not hear the half of what you said." I said, " Yes, you said so ; but I am not referring to what *I* said but what *you* said *yourself*. Now, Archibald, did you not say these words to me ? " He answered, " Mr. Bethune, I did not hear the half of what you said ; I was cold and I am dull of hearing." I replied again, " I am not asking you about what I said, but what you said yourself. You would surely hear yourself. Tell me, now, did you not say so ? " He replied, " Mr. Bethune, upon my word I did not hear the half of what you said." To which I answered, " That will do, Archibald ; you know you said so, and you have not the heart to deny it. You are always *evading* my question. I am not asking what I said to you, which you might not hear well, but what you said to me. You heard of course what you said yourself; but you don't want to own it now after voting for that letter." So much for one of those I had referred to.

The above faithful narrative on the actual merits of that letter in question shows how a man's veracity can be called in question without cause; all the more inexcusable in this case as the scandalous conduct it sought to cover from those who had not seen it, and, by implication, to insinuate as a fabrication of ours, was so extraordinary and outrageous as in the whole community who saw it—Baptists as well as others—there was and only could be but one opinion, that it was *a very great* scandal and disgrace. Many with myself felt ashamed of it for the discredit it was fitted to bring on the Christian religion in general. I don't expect ever to see its like again. At least we sincerely hope so. It is a pleasure to us that both of the meetings in our own church, which were very largely attended, were in quietness and order all that could be desired, and that while we spoke plainly we were careful to show all courtesy and fairness.

IV.

The last of the letters referred to, which I have seen, appeared in the *Canadian Baptist*, of 20th April, from the Rev. Mr. McNeill of Paisley, or on the same day that as already explained my reply to the Rev. Mr. McDonald's was refused publication there; by which any other replies I might be inclined to send in self-defence, were of course equally excluded. Mr. McN's. was in correction of a statement of mine about himself in a previous issue. D. McG. in his of the 9th March, among its other things had represented me as saying about Mr. McN. at a meeting here, what was as different in nature and words from what I had said, as night is from day, and in my reply I corrected that point by stating what I did say. At the meeting in question among other illustrations of unworthy modes of proselytism, I mentioned one as *recently* related to me by a person who was the subject of it, and whom, as she bore a respectable character, I believed. She afterwards again verified to me its correctness. Mr. McN. however in his letter denied it fully, and explained the facts. Besides this, he said, " I hold Mr. Bethune responsible for it all, not the young woman;" that is, that I invented the whole myself! To impress his readers that I was very active in seeking to injure him in the matter, he stated that I " published it in one of the Walkerton papers," etc., and he " cannot imagine where or when I am going to end it." I published it in no Walkerton or *any other* paper or place, but only as above mentioned. Now suppose of that misstatement of his, I were to follow his example and say, ' I hold him responsible for it all, not anyone else ?' But I will not be so *unjust*, as I presume he has been wrongly informed, and, believing it, has repeated it to his readers of me as true. He further describes me to them as one who " sanctimoniously subscribes himself, ' The Presbyterian Minister of Chesley ;'" and remarks that he "had no apprehension that the charges would to any serious extent damage his reputation, *considering especially their source*;" that is, considering especially what kind of a person I am known to be. Such and other like language he has chosen to use of a minister of whom he knows little, and against whose personal character he certainly never knew anything unprincipled, though not without its share, doubtless, of the imperfections common to all Christians. To such statements I make no reply, but that I have no doubt they will be regarded as quite inapplicable and improper by all around who know us, with all our shortcomings. That statement of mine, however, I am free to say in the interests of truth and justice, I regard as in the first place an indiscretion on my part. Being on the subject of proselytism, (of unworthy methods of which I knew a good many genuine instances of different places, and who does not?) I related this in a moment of warmth; simply from happening to have been informed of it but two weeks before by one I deemed trustworthy, which was therefore fresh in my mind. I had before in the Baptist church (17th Dec.), mentioned another instance of a flagrant kind in our immediate neighbourhood, the principle actor of it being present, (who smiled as it was referred to,) which has not been denied. It also was known to me only by testimony, (on which we must depend entirely for much of our knowledge,) but was not strictly private. The case in question, however, being of a private conversation, had

in its nature only one witness. Yet from this circumstance,
if denied, it could not be satisfactorily established however
true; and there was the *possibility* of its not being correct
after all, and of doing injustice. The Scripture rule is
clearly the only safe one, "In the mouth of two or three
witnesses let every word be established." But also from
Mr. McNiell's explanation of the facts, which looked like
the truth and from subsequent corroboration, it seems to
me I have been misled, and that he has been really misrepresented in that matter; which I sincerely and much
regret. And I now take the first suitable opportunity I
have had of acknowledging this and much more widely
than the statement complained of, including those, doubtless, to whom it was first made. Although, however, from
the action of the *Canadian Baptist* Editor in then excluding
my replies, who of course knew nothing of how far the
communications he did publish were true or untrue; and
from the grossly unwarrantable abuse Mr. McN. chose to
add over and above his own defence there, I might fairly
not have noticed the matter here; as certainly he unjustly
said, and to those who would too readily believe all, much
more unworthy things of me than my statement contained
of him. I may here repeat *its* burden, which was, viz.,
"that after the young woman in answer to his inquiry had
said that she did not consider herself converted yet, he
then asked her if she was not thinking of joining the church
(his own church by immersion understood), adding, that
she knew if she wished the blessing she must use the
means." Besides the specimens from his letter already
given, he also remarked that he could " scarcely believe
nature so bad that she could invent or make such misstatements except they were elicited" by " the solicitations
of her minister." In other words that I " solicited " her
to "invent" false statements! What a man, what a
minister must his Baptist readers suppose us to be,—capable of such conduct! From the different epithets, etc.,
used by him, it will be seen that my chastiser has wielded
a heavy club, felling down his unfortunate Infant Baptist
brother to the ground with every stroke; but whether in
the spirit of the divine exhortation, "Render to no man
evil for evil," and of Him "who when he was reviled reviled not again," we leave him and others to judge. It

will be seen from this case, however, that to misrepresent a Baptist, however unintentionally, and fall into his power by an indiscretion, is a very serious matter in practice. On the other hand what shall we think of the numberless misrepresentations of every kind of us, intentionally heaped from that side by those who unquestionably knew better? But Mr. McN. perhaps from a habit of speaking strongly where the question of Baptism is concerned, (which is the case with many) against Infant Baptists, and strongly sensitive where himself is misrepresented, may not have meant all that his words convey, or would not use them in calmer mind. To that we are all too liable. I do not know him personally, but from, what I have heard of him, I yet incline to respect him withal. In this case I believe he has received some provocation, and forgive him, all the more readily on that account, what he has said amiss of me. His, and now my references to the case may do us both good, and others, in making us more careful of what we say and do. My exhibition of the preceeding letters may do some good similarly, as well as otherwise; though it is to be expected that dishonest unscrupulous spirits will go on purposely misrepresenting where it may best serve their object, especially so long as the practice, of highly immoral tendency, prevails, of Editors' publishing communications with personal accusations without the personal signature of the writers, which allows and therefore attracts such spirits to take advantage of the opportunities thus afforded without fear of being made answerable personally. And this will be all the more indulged in where in addition it is found that replies in correction and defence from the accused do not appear; because *quietly kept back* by editors more influenced by party sectarian policy than regard for truth and justice between man and man.

But apart from this case the practice of unworthy methods of proselytism is notorious all over the country; on which the first half of this book gives some evidence in the argumentative line, and the appendices, etc., in others; with which the extracts from Bunyan, in the preface, of the practice in his times quite agree.

In these appendices local matters have been dwelt on, which while they have their own instruction and value on the general question, yet do not themselves decide its merits. They show, indeed, what a man may expect, who even on a small scale and in circumstances that call much for it, endeavours, however respectfully in manner, to defend what we believe the truth in opposition to their ideas. The more successful he may be in this, he may expect to fare the harder, judging from our experience, which by the way is not uncommon. But on the general question we have set before you evidence from a wider area, viz., the systematic misrepresentation in books issued by the central Publication Societies of the Baptist Church in Canada, the United States, etc., from one generation to another, with the historical evidence on the subject, etc., we have laid before you of the genuine facts from *Baptist* and other sources.

For my own part, I can conscientiously say, I have not intentionally misrepresented throughout all our proceedings any person or thing. And I may add: if any of my readers, at hand, who have not the books quoted from in this treatise, desire to see them for verification, and call on me, I will be happy to afford the facility. May the Lord bless all in every denomination who love the Lord Jesus in sincerity; and add to their number constantly. O the happy time, when all his people will see eye to eye, and he will have healed the breaches of Zion; may it come quickly! Amen. Meanwhile, let Christians seek more and more grace from above to obey the divine exhortation to all his people: "Let all bitterness, and wrath, and anger, and clamour, and evil-speaking, be put away from among you, with all malice; and be ye kind one to another, tender-hearted, forgiving one another, even as God for Christ's sake has forgiven you." O blissful heaven, where there is no sin within nor around, but the rest that remaineth for the people of God! Reader, are you on your way thither? If not, strive to enter in at the strait gate to it. Jesus is both the *door* and the *way*. Believe on, take up thy cross, and follow Him.

FINIS.